# The Successful Sales Meetings Handbook

By Bill N. Newman

www.sunvillagepublications.com

The Successful Sales Meetings Handbook
By Bill N. Newman

Copyright © 2011

No part of this publication may be reproduced, stored in a retrieval system or transmitted in any form or by any means, electronic, mechanical, photocopying, recording or otherwise, without prior written permission from the publisher.

Disclaimer: Neither the author nor the publisher accepts any responsibility for any injury, damage, or unwanted or adverse circumstances or conditions arising from use or misuse of the material contained within this publication. While every effort has been made to ensure reliability and accuracy of the information within, the liability, negligence or otherwise, or from any use, misuse or abuse arising the operation of any methods, strategies, instructions or ideas contained in the material herein is the sole responsibility of the reader.

Cover photo credits: © Wavebreakmedia Ltd/Dreamstime.com

www.sunvillagepublications.com

Cover design by www.WebCopyAlchemy.com

# Contents

| CHAPTER | PAGE |
|---|---|

**1. What Good Sales Meetings Will Do for You** . . . . . 1

    SEVEN WAYS TO CASH IN ON MEETINGS BY INCREASING SALES    2

        1. You *Can* Improve *Communications.* 2. You Can *Introduce New Policies and Products.* 3. Your Sales Staff Can Be Instructed and Trained. *4.* Your Sales Staff Can Be Motivated. 5. You Can Exchange Ideas *with Your* Staff. 6. You Can Lead Your Staff *in Creative Thinking.* 7. You Can Solve Problems.

    THE BIGGEST PAY OFF OF ALL . . . . . . . . 6

**2. How to Plan Your Sales Meetings** . . . . . . . 8

    HOW TO DETERMINE THE OBJECTIVE OF YOUR MEETING . . 8
    HOW TO GIVE YOUR AUDIENCE WHAT IT WANTS . . . . 9
    HOW TO PREPARE YOUR AGENDA . . . . . . . 10
    HOW TO ARRANGE YOUR SUBJECT MATTER . . . . 10
    SAMPLE AGENDA . . . . . . . . . . 10
    HOW TO DECIDE UPON THE LENGTH OF YOUR MEETING . . 11
    HOW TO SELECT THE BEST TIME FOR YOUR MEETINGS . . . 12
    HOW TO CHOOSE THE PERSONNEL TO ATTEND YOUR MEETING    12
    PLAN A POSITIVE TONE FOR YOUR MEETING . . . . 13
    A CASE IN POINT . . . . . . . . . . 14

**3. How to Build Your Meetings Around a Central Theme** . . 16

    USE DEMONSTRATION NOT CONVERSATION . . . . 16
    HOW TO SELECT AN APPROPRIATE THEME . . . . 17
    HOW TO APPLY YOUR CENTRAL THEME . . . . 17
    THEME—ROUNDUP. TYPE OF SELLING—JOBBING OR
        WHOLESALE . . . . . . . . . 18

3. **How to Build Your Meetings Around a Central Theme (continued)**

 Theme—April Showers. Type of Selling—Over the
  Counter . . . . . . . . . . 19
 Theme—Sales Fever. Type of Selling—Any Type . . . 20
 52 Themes You Can Use . . . . . . . . 21
 Have Speakers Use the Language of Your Theme . . 23
 Plan Decorations That Coincide with Your Theme . . 23
 Arrange Entertainment That Fits Your Theme . . . 23
 Serve Refreshments That Project Your Theme . . . 24
 Use Announcements That Carry Out Your Theme . . 24

4. **How to Use Variety and Showmanship** . . . . 26

 Salespeople Demand the Best . . . . . 26
 Rotate Chairmanship of the Meetings to Create
  Variety . . . . . . . . . . .27
 How to Use a Seminar to Vary the Routine . . . . 28
 How to Use a Panel Discussion . . . . . . 29
 How to Use Experts in an Unusual Way. . . . . 30
 How to Use Discussion Groups. . . . . . . 31
 How to Use Interpreters. . . . . . . . 31
 How to Stage the Courtroom Plan. . . . . . 31
 How to Make Use of the Competitive Instinct . . . 32
 How to Add Variety Through Costuming. . . . . 33
 Outside Speakers Can Be Effective. . . . . . 33
 How to Use a Mind Reading Act. . . . . . . 33
 Startle Them with a Coroner's Inquest. . . . . .34
 Consider the Occasional Use of Entertainment . . . 35
 Conduct Interviews with Members of the Audience . . 35
 Provide a Goal at Which to Shoot. . . . . . 36
 Quiz Programs Get Points Across. . . . . . 37
 How to Use Contests to Spice Your Meetings . . . 38
 How to Use the Element of Suspense. . . . . . 38
 Planned Interruptions Produce a Change of Pace . . 39
 How to Use Skits to Keep Interest. . . . . . 39
 Six Skits You Can Use. . . . . . . . 40

CONTENTS                                                          vii

4. **How to Use Variety and Showmanship (continued)**

   BORROW FROM THE THEATER.         .     .     .     .     41
   HOW TO USE GIVEAWAYS EFFECTIVELY.     .     .     .     42
   HOW TO HIT THE JACKPOT.     .     .     .     .     .    42
   LET THEM TELL ABOUT THE BENEFITS.     .     .     .     43
   HOW TO USE A CORPORATE "CHARACTER".     .     .     .    .43
   VARIETY IS THE SPICE OF LIFE.     .     .     .     .    44

5. **How to Use Audio-Visual Aids Effectively.**     .     .     **45**

   MOVIES AND FILMSTRIPS ARE OFTEN MISUSED.     .     .    45
   MANY FIRMS PRODUCE THEIR OWN FILMS.     .     .     .    .46
   WHERE TO FIND THE GREATEST SOURCE OF AUDIO-VISUAL
     AIDS.     .     .     .     .     .     .     .     .     47
   TEST YOUR PROJECTION EQUIPMENT BEFOREHAND.     .     .   47
   TIMING IS IMPORTANT.     .     .     .     .     .     . 48
   DEVELOP A COMPETENT PROJECTIONIST.     .     .     .     .49
   WHAT TO DO AFTER THE SHOWING.     .     .     .     .    49
   HOW TO USE THE OPAQUE PROJECTOR.     .     .     .     . .50
   THE VERSATILE OVERHEAD PROJECTOR.     .     .     .     .50
   HOW TO USE THE CHALKBOARD.     .     .     .     .     . 50
   EIGHT TIPS FOR USING CHALKBOARDS EFFECTIVELY.     .     .51
   GENERATED CHARTS MAY SUBSTITUTE FOR CHALKBOARDS.    .  51
   HOW TO USE PREPARED CHARTS.     .     .     .     .     52
   HOW TO BUILD YOUR POINTS USING A SLAP BOARD.     .     . 52
   THE FLOCK BOARD IS AN INNOVATION.     .     .     .     .53
   SIX SUGGESTIONS FOR USING SLAP BOARDS.     .     .     . 53
   HOW TO USE A TAPE RECORDER PROFITABLY.     .     .     ..53
   DISPLAYS CREATE THE RIGHT MOOD.     .     .     .     .  54
   AUDIO-VISUAL AIDS ARE INVALUABLE—USE THEM .     .     .  55

6. **How to Use Speakers to Best Advantage.**     .     .     .     **57**

   MINIMIZE THE AMOUNT OF SPEAKING.     .     .     .     . 57
   HOW TO SELECT THE RIGHT SPEAKERS.     .     .     .     58
   ROTATE THE SPEAKING ASSIGNMENTS.     .     .     .     ..58
   SHORT TALKS ARE BETTER THAN LONG ONES.     .     .     ..59
   PLACE YOUR STRONGEST SPEAKERS AT CRUCIAL SPOTS .     .   59

## 6. How to Use Speakers to Best Advantage (continued)

KEEP THE SUBJECTS IN LOGICAL SEQUENCE. . . . . 59
PRODUCE A CHANGE OF PACE. . . . . . . . . 60
HOW TO GET SPEAKERS TO PREPARE. . . . . . . 60
HOW TO HELP YOUR SPEAKERS. . . . . . . . 60
WHAT EVERY SPEAKER SHOULD KNOW ABOUT FEAR . . . 61
THE CAUSE OF FEAR. . . . . . . . . . . 61
15 WAYS TO COMBAT FEAR. . . . . . . . . 62
HOW TO KEEP THE ATTENTION OF A LARGE AUDIENCE . . 66
HOW A SPEAKER CAN PROJECT HIS VOICE. . . . . 66
WHEN TO USE VOICE PROJECTION. . . . . . . 67

## 7. How to Organize a Speech. . . . . . . . . 68

HOW TO COLLECT MATERIAL FOR A TALK. . . . . 68
HOW TO DECIDE UPON THE POINT OF A TALK. . . . 69
HOW TO DETERMINE WHETHER THE POINT IS APPROPRIATE . 69
HOW TO DEVELOP THE MEAT OF A TALK . . . . . 70
HOW TO PREPARE THE CLOSE OF A TALK. . . . . 70
HOW TO WORK OUT THE BEGINNING OF A TALK. . . . 71
A BIRD'S-EYE VIEW OF THE FIVE-STEP PLAN. . . . 71
WHY THE FIVE-STEP PLAN IS SO EFFECTIVE. . . . . 72
HOW AUDIENCE REACTION IS TAKEN INTO ACCOUNT . . . 72
SIMPLICITY MAKES IT EASY TO USE. . . . . . . 73
IT'S ALSO THE NATURAL THING TO DO. . . . . . 79
HOW TO PUT ACROSS MORE THAN ONE POINT. . . . 79
HOW TO GET YOUR SPEAKERS TO USE THE PLAN . . . 79

## 8. How to Put Humor Into a Speech. . . . . . . 81

HOW TO BECOME A GOOD STORY TELLER. . . . . 81
MAN'S INHUMANITY TO MAN. . . . . . . . . 82
A NATURAL TARGET. . . . . . . . . . . 83
THE UNEXPECTED. . . . . . . . . . . 84
SEX. . . . . . . . . . . . . . . 84
HOW TO HAVE A DOUBLE BARREL APPEAL. . . . . 85
HOW TO HANDLE THE PUNCH LINE. . . . . . . 86

# CONTENTS

## 8. How to Put Humor Into a Speech (continued)

How to Find Humor for a Talk. . . . . . . 86
How to Relate Humor to Your Other Material . . 87
Be Careful of the Tendency to Associate. . . . . 89

## 9. Forty-Five Ways to Put Life Into a Speech. . . . . .91

The Appeal to Basic Emotions and Urges. . . . . 91
How to Improve Your Speakers and Speeches . . . 92
How to Add Showmanship to Any Talk. . . . . 93
How to Use Costuming. . . . . . . . .94
How to Make a Talk Light and Interesting. . . . 94
How to Cover Basic Fundamentals Effectively . . 96
How to Dramatize Mental Attitude. . . . . . 97
How to Bring the Law of Averages to Life . . . . 98
How to Dramatize Systematic Prospecting. . . . 99
How to Present the Customer's Point of View . . 100
How to Show Loss or Gain. . . . . . . . 100
How to Act Out Various Points. . . . . . 101
How to Make Your Speakers Get Hot. . . . . 101
How to Arrange Timely Interruptions. . . . .102
How to Animate Speeches with Cross-Overs . . . 103
When to Have Your Speakers Destroy Their Notes 104

## 10. How to make Good Physical Arrangements . . . . . . . . . . . . . . . 106

How to Locate Desirable Meeting Rooms . . . . 106
How to Arrange for Meals. . . . . . . . 107
How to Choose the Best Meeting Room. . . . 108
Be Certain to Inspect the Room. . . . . . . 109
Pros and Cons of Seating Arrangements. . . . .
109
Poor Acoustics Are Murder. . . . . . . . 111
Guard Against Alien Noises. . . . . . . . 111
Anticipate All Physical Needs Before Selecting a
Room. . . . . . . . . . . . 111
How to Select the Best "Mike" for Your Purpose . 112
Last-Minute Details to Check. . . . . . . 114

## CONTENTS

**11. How to Ensure a Good Audience.** . . . . . . . . . **115**

    How to Put Sales Meetings on a Positive Plane . .   115
    How to Use the Magic of Music. . . . . . . . 116
    Get Them Acquainted with Each Other. . . . . 116
    How to Start Your Meetings on Time. . . . . 117
    How to Create Informality. . . . . . . . .118
    How to Make Money Talk. . . . . . . . .119
    How to Make Them Want to Listen. . . . . 120
    How to Stay on Schedule. . . . . . . . .120
    How to Use a Timing Device. . . . . . . .121
    The Value of Using a Timekeeper. . . . . 122

**12. How to Emcee a Sales Meeting.** . . . . . **124**

    16 Ways to Be a Good Emcee. . . . . . . 124

        J. Be rehearsed. 2. Anticipate *pitfalls.* 3. Be alive, vibrant. 4. *Refrain from apologizing.* 5. Introduce speakers properly. 6. *Wait for the* speaker *to get there.* 7. *Assist the speaker.* 8. Show your own interest. 9. Don't remake a speech. 10. Use humor. 11. *Make everyone feel important.* 12. Get, and keep, participation. 13. *Make light of disturbances.* 14. *Keep it under control.* 15. *Make it move.* 16. *Give credits before the climax.*

**13. How to Climax Your Sales Meeting.** . . . . . . . **131**

    Every Sales Meeting Should Be Climaxed . . . . 131
    Facts About Semi climaxes. . . . . . . . .132
    How to Guard Against an Anticlimax. . . . . 132
    14 Ways to Climax a Sales Meeting. . . . . . .
    133

**14. How to Conduct Group Training Sessions.** . . . . **138**

    How to Teach Groups Effectively. . . . . . 138
    Prepare Your Audience. . . . . . . . .139
    Present Your Material. . . . . . . . 139
    Have Them Learn by Doing. . . . . . . 140
    Check on Learning. . . . . . . . . . 140
    Appeal to as Many Senses as Possible. . . . 141

## CONTENTS

**14. How to Conduct Group Training Sessions (continued)**

    HOW TO SUGARCOAT YOUR TRAINING. . . . . 141
    10 WAYS TO MAKE SALES TRAINING MORE INTERESTING . 142
    HOW TO USE TRUE-FALSE TESTS. . . . . . .146
    SAMPLE QUIZ ON APPROACHES. . . . . . . . 146

**15. How to Publicize Your Sales Meetings. . . . . 148**

    HOW TO PREPARE PROMOTIONAL LEAFLETS. . . . . 149
    HOW TO PREPARE PROMOTIONAL LETTERS. . . . . . 149
    HOW TO USE THE SIX MAJOR NEWS ANGLES. . . . . 151
    HOW TO TIME YOUR NEWSPAPER RELEASES. . . . . 153
    HOW TO PREPARE YOUR NEWSPAPER RELEASES . . . . 153
    HOW TO SUBMIT YOUR NEWSPAPER RELEASES . . . . 156
    HOW TO GET EXTRA NEWSPAPER COVERAGE. . . . . 156

**16. How to Conduct Special Type Sales Meetings . . . . 158**

    HOW TO CONDUCT A PROBLEM SOLVING CONFERENCE . . 158
    20 WAYS TO BE A GOOD CONFERENCE LEADER . . . . 160
    HOW TO ORGANIZE A WORKSHOP. . . . . . .162
    PROBLEMS CAN BE OF A POSITIVE NATURE. . . . . 163
    MOST PEOPLE WILL SUGGEST PROBLEMS THAT ARE
        NEGATIVE. . . . . . . . . . . 163
    HOW TO APPOINT COMMITTEES. . . . . . .164
    HOW TO CONDUCT A WORKSHOP. . . . . . .164
    HOW TO SELECT A SUBJECT FOR BRAIN STORMING . . . 165
    HOW TO CONDUCT A BRAIN STORMING SESSION . . . . 165
    HOW TO MAKE BRAIN STORMING PAY DIVIDENDS . . . 166
    HOW TO CONDUCT A BUZZ SESSION. . . . . . . 167
    HOW TO GIVE BUZZ SESSIONS AN INTERESTING TWIST . . 168

**17. How to Conduct a Recruiting Meeting. . . . . 170**

    EIGHT WAYS TO GET PROSPECTIVE SALESPEOPLE TO A
        RECRUITING MEETING. . . . . . . . .171
    WHERE TO CONDUCT YOUR RECRUITING MEETING . . . 176
    HOW TO RECEIVE THE PROSPECTIVE SALESPEOPLE . . . 177

## 17. How to Conduct a Recruiting Meeting (continued)

    HOW TO PLAN A RECRUITING MEETING. . . . . . . 178
    SAMPLE AGENDA. . . . . . . . . . 178
    HOW TO HOLD THE PSYCHOLOGICAL UPPER HAND . . . 181
    HOW TO HANG OUT THE DOLLAR SIGN. . . . . . 181

## 18. How to Conduct a Large Meeting or Convention . . . 183

    HOW TO MAKE ANOTHER PERSON RESPONSIBLE . . . . 183
    HOW TO SELECT A STEERING COMMITTEE. . . . . 184
    SAMPLE CHECK LIST FOR PHYSICAL ARRANGEMENTS
        COMMITTEE. . . . . . . . . . . 185
    CHECK LIST FOR BUDGET AND FINANCE COMMITTEE . . 186
    CHECK LIST FOR PROMOTION AND PUBLICITY COMMITTEE 187
    CHECK LIST FOR DECORATION COMMITTEE. . . . . 188
    CHECK LIST FOR REGISTRATION COMMITTEE. . . . . 189
    CHECK LIST FOR RECEPTION AND ENTERTAINMENT
        COMMITTEE. . . . . . . . . . . .191
    CHECK LIST FOR PROGRAM COMMITTEE. . . . . . 192
    CHECK LIST FOR BANQUET COMMITTEE. . . . . . 195
    ACCIDENTS CAN HAPPEN. . . . . . . . . 196
    HOW TO PROTECT YOURSELF AND YOUR COMPANY . . . 196

## 19. How to Evaluate Your Sales Meetings. . . . . . .197

    HOW TO OBTAIN THE EVALUATION REPORT. . . . . 197
    POST MEETING ANALYSIS. . . . . . . . 198
    EVALUATION REPORT. . . . . . . . . 198
    POST MEETING REACTION REPORT. . . . . . 199
    HOW TO ANALYZE THE EVALUATION REPORTS . . . . 200
    THE BEST EVALUATION OF ALL. . . . . . 201

**Index**. . . . . . . . . . . .203

# 1. What Good Sales Meetings Will Do for You

There's a sales meeting somewhere. Morning, noon, or night—a sales meeting is taking place. There are more this year than last, and next year there'll be more than ever. Sales meetings are popular because of one thing . . . they pay dividends! They're often the difference between profit and loss, the difference between success and failure. Sales meetings are that important.

Meetings can work wonders for the people attending. After a snappy meeting in Akron, Ohio, a salesman remarked, "I learned more about selling in one hour than I had in the last year!" Another commented, "I always get 'pumped up' when I go to sales meetings. I'd be lost without them."

Good sales meetings are profitable for all concerned. However a sales meeting must actually be *good* for everyone to benefit. If there's reason to believe a meeting will not be successful, improve your plans . . . or don't stage the meeting. If there's doubt about the need for a meeting, establish the need . . . or don't call the meeting.

A poor meeting is torture. Even a mediocre meeting is not acceptable. An effective sales meeting is instructional and inspirational, both interesting and exciting. Everyone attending becomes a participant, at least in spirit. They accept and approve, nodding their heads in agreement with the speakers and demonstrations.

# WHAT *GOOD SALES MEETINGS WILL DO*

**Seven Ways to Cash in on Meetings by Increasing Sales**

1. You Can Improve Communications.

Modern business is complex. It calls for specialization, each worker being a small cog in the machinery. This makes it more difficult for an employee to see the overall picture. The need for communications, then, has become greater.

Keep channels of communication open. Unexplained intentions are usually considered evil. "Unless there's something wrong with the deal, why don't they let us in on it?"

Several salesmen left their jobs with a furniture manufacturer. Finally the cause was explained: "We thought we'd be let out," stated one of the men. "Everybody knew sales were off and that a new owner was taking over." Unfortunately, the men were victims of rumor. Sales were off but little. Profits were as high as ever, and the new owner intended to keep the sales personnel intact.

There's a "grapevine" in every company. Telephone conversations are overheard, letters are read by typists and file clerks. Information leaks out sooner or later. Let workers get the story straight. Let them get it from you. What you tell them will be much more accurate than what they hear from each other.

Although you should communicate with all employees, it's especially important to communicate with salespeople. Your sales staff is in constant contact with the public. When you communicate with salesmen, you communicate with many people.

For instance, your salesmen are in constant contact with customers. When you communicate with salesmen, you are indirectly communicating with customers.

2. **You Can Introduce** *New Policies and Products.*

Any major change, such as the introduction of a new policy, can be discussed at a sales meeting. By calling your men together, you attach importance to the event, moreover, you can show exactly how the new matter is to be handled.

Good personnel practices suggest that changes be explained in advance. This makes a change more acceptable. Sometimes

# WHAT *GOOD SALES MEETINGS WILL DO* 3

it is advisable to go a step further and sell your staff on the change. Sales meetings are good for both you and your staff. You can explain proposed policy so those affected will know they've been considered. And you can sell the change, causing all concerned to accept it.

3. Your Sales Staff Can Be *Instructed and Trained.*

Of the many benefits that come from sales meetings, instruction and training stand out.

"You've gotta tell 'em how and show 'em how," exclaimed the field sales manager of a milling concern. "Then have 'em practice it. These things can best be accomplished in group meetings."

Sales meetings offer a time-tested opportunity for training your salesmen. A great deal of information can be put across to many people in a short time.

What is the purpose of a sales meeting? Generally, sales meetings are conducted for the benefit of those who attend. But let's talk about you and how *you* can benefit from good sales meetings.

## Sales Meetings Increase Sales

Your greatest benefit will be an increase in sales. While this increase cannot always be measured, it is the main reason for having meetings and the natural result of good meetings. You should expect an increase in sales. If necessary, you should insist upon it.

The Sales Manager of an Eastern concern stated, "We've tried 'em all—contests, push periods, red-letter days—everything from Christmas bonuses to a founder's day banquet. But the best way to stimulate sales is by meetings—regular and well planned sales meetings."

A case in point: a chain system of variety stores had few meetings. "Most stores had monthly get-togethers," a vice president reported. "And to be honest about it, those monthly meetings were sometimes skipped. But last year we insisted on weekly meetings—good weekly meetings. And sales increased 16 percent, apparently for that reason alone."

## 4 WHAT *GOOD* SALES MEETINGS WILL *DO*

So there's good reason to use the information in the following chapters. Your sales volume is a cinch to zoom upward!

4. Your Sales Staff Can Be Motivated.

Is your sales plan effective? Do you offer a quality product or service? Are your sales personnel well trained?

A sales manager might say "Yes" to the foregoing questions. Even so, another ingredient is also vital. Motivation is needed. His staff must be motivated to carry out the sales plan, to offer the product or service, to use the training they've received.

Good sales meetings can bring about this motivation that is so necessary. Having been made more capable of doing his job, a salesman is more willing. And has more confidence and enthusiasm.

Some firms have a brief sales meeting every day—yes, every day! The reason: motivation. A pep talk or two at the beginning of each day generates heavy sales activity.

5. You Can Exchange Ideas with Your Staff.

An exchange of information is usually quite profitable. Firms over the country have reported a long list of benefits.

- .... It acts as a safety valve for employees' feelings. Why let emotions be stifled until the boiling point is reached?
- .... Misunderstandings are cleared up. This makes for greater harmony throughout the organization.
- .... You can check on employee training. A salesman is not necessarily trained even though he has been exposed to training.
- .... Persons recently absent can be brought up to date.
- .... Errors in sales strategy are prevented. Thus sales are made that otherwise would have been lost.
- .... Systems and procedures can be improved. For instance, there may be a better method of merchandise control . . . or of merchandise display.
- .... Plans can be coordinated. This eliminates duplication of effort. It also precludes wide gaps in planning.
- .... Salesmen are made to feel important. Inferiority complexes are minimized.

# WHAT *GOOD SALES MEETINGS WILL DO* 5

.... The men gain confidence because of their increased knowledge and speak to customers with greater conviction.

.... Having learned more about their fellow workers, the men gain new respect for each other, reducing friction.

.... Teamwork becomes smoother since employees are more willing to work with each other. And better teamwork can increase sales or lower the cost of selling, or both.

.... Loyalty to management is developed as management becomes better understood. Salesmen are willing to work harder and longer.

.... Turnover is reduced. A happy and well-informed worker is less likely to go to work for a competitor.

Yes, all this can be accomplished in sales meetings—and more. Small meetings conducted by a sympathetic supervisor can bring a valuable exchange of ideas.

6. You *Can Lead* Your Staff in Creative Thinking.

It's said that we use only 10 percent of our mental capacities. True or not—most of us do little creative thinking. We're too involved with routine matters.

Ever done any brainstorming? Brainstorming is a specialized type of sales meeting. The purpose of it is to stimulate creative thinking. One creative thought might eliminate your greatest problem! A single new idea might double or triple your sales volume!

A fellow in Duluth, Minnesota, stated, "My prior associates worked together at solving problems but did no creative thinking. Here at this company we have regular meetings involving creative thinking. They're both satisfying and rewarding."

Brainstorming has paid off for many sales executives. It can pay off for you.

7. **You Can *Solve Problems.***

Group thinking is widely used in business today as a means of solving complex problems. Many firms have increased sales, while others have reduced selling costs, and some have done both.

It's easy to stage a problem solving conference. One person

suggests the first step toward solving a problem. The next missing link is provided by another person. Someone else fills in the third gap, and before long a solution is reached.

One of the nation's leading airlines arranged for regular problem solving conferences years ago. The director of operations said, "Every major problem involves more than one member of the staff. Why not let all concerned, tackle it together?"

### The Biggest Pay Off of All

It is hoped that many sales executives will benefit personally from the ten-year collection of "how to" information contained in this book. Some may get promotions due to it.

The president of a large corporation declared, "If there's any one ability that makes a man stand out, it's the ability to conduct sales meetings."

When you conduct a meeting you show what you know about public speaking, human relations, employee training, showmanship, selling, and sales management—to mention but a few! The fellow who conducts good sales meetings is always in demand. He can get a job, a better job, a pay raise.

Perhaps you're the owner of a company and, thus, are not seeking advancement. In your case, the opportunity to increase sales may be your greatest interest. There can still be personal benefit, however. There's the benefit that comes from being a strong leader ... from *deceiving* respect instead of commanding it. Someone said, "The boss may not be right, but he's still the boss." That's true. But he can be the boss and be right too! There's satisfaction in doing a big job the right way—in spite of the fact that you're the boss!

**WHAT GOOD SALES MEETINGS WILL DO FOR YOU**

**Increase Sales**

**Improve Communications**

**Help Introduce New Policies and Products**

**Facilitate Group Training**

# WHAT *GOOD SALES MEETINGS WILL DO*      7

    **Motivate Your Salespeople**

    **Act as an Idea Exchange**

    **Stimulate Creative Thinking**

    **Result in Problem Solving**

    **Provide Personal Benefits**

# 2. How to Plan Your Sales Meetings

Good sales meetings are like good sales. They don't just happen. They are made to happen.

"I don't see any visitors on Fridays," declared the sales manager of a large real estate firm, "Most of every Friday is devoted to planning my Saturday morning sales meetings." Such thorough planning is more than a good investment. It's absolutely essential for a good meeting.

"We have regular monthly meetings," explained a Minneapolis department store owner. "The moment one meeting is over, we start planning the next. There's a critique after every meeting. At that time we discuss what to do, and what not to do, at our meeting the following month."

**HOW TO DETERMINE THE OBJECTIVE OF YOUR MEETING**

The first step in planning a sales meeting is to decide on an objective.

How can your personnel do a bigger and better job? If you analyzed sales records, could you spot areas in which there's room for improvement? For instance, would the records show a need for more calls? How about new items—are they being "pushed"? Can selling costs be lowered?

Other company officials may have suggestions. Should they be queried? Does the director of marketing believe your salesmen are in tune with current trends? Can the advertising manager

# HOW TO PLAN YOUR SALES MEETINGS

suggest better ways to use advertising at the point of sale? Does the personnel manager have anything to "throw in the pot"? How about the merchandise manager?

The manager of a drugstore chain asked himself questions such as these. He was surprised at the answers he received! Several staff members had suggestions, all of real benefit. A post meeting reaction report revealed that the sales people considered the meeting to be the most helpful they had ever attended.

Decide what should be accomplished. Aim for specific objectives. Do you want to inform everyone? Do you want to tell of impending changes? Or do you want to cover certain problems? Is motivation the prime objective? If so, in what way? Should your staff be inspired to work harder? Longer? Do you want to exchange ideas or is specific training needed? What should be done?

Finally . . . is a sales meeting the best means of accomplishing your objective? What do you want your sales staff to do as a result of the meeting? Do you want more enthusiasm shown? More call backs now?

### HOW TO GIVE YOUR AUDIENCE WHAT IT WANTS

So much for your objective. What does the audience hope to accomplish?

Many members of the audience will have their own objectives. Some will want one thing, while others will want another. One individual may desire certain product information, for example. Another might be seeking the answer to a new objection.

Group discussion will satisfy many of these specific needs. *However, the major need oi the audience is a good meeting.* Make the meeting interesting, enjoyable, and beneficial. Everyone would gladly settle for that! Make each meeting so interesting, enjoyable and beneficial that the audience will welcome the next.

Occasionally you should poll the audience. Hand out pieces of paper headed, "Subjects to be covered at future sales meetings." Some of the suggestions that are listed will surprise you! By covering most of their requests, however, you'll be giving the audience the subjects desired. Most of their topics will be good ones, too.

### HOW TO PREPARE YOUR AGENDA

To prepare an agenda, select topics in keeping with the objective.

If you want to motivate salesmen, what subjects would be most likely to do it? Wouldn't something on enthusiasm be inspirational? What about positive thinking? Should you have someone give an account of how he succeeded?

Let's suppose you want to train instead of motivate. In what areas is training needed? On product information? On closing techniques? Can training needs be satisfied at one meeting or should a series of meetings be scheduled? Which training needs are most important? For example, isn't it all important for every man to master his sales presentation? Which needs are most urgent? Shouldn't you do something now to get the men to move overstocked items?

Ask yourself questions such as these. You can then decide upon appropriate subject matter.

### HOW TO ARRANGE YOUR SUBJECT MATTER

Items for the agenda should be arranged in logical sequence. Tips on approaching the customer are placed before methods of presenting the product. A demonstration of the product should precede closing the sale.

The sales vice president of an industrial concern said, "A natural sequence makes for better understanding. Schedule any general information first. Then narrow the subject matter toward your objective, becoming more specific all the time."

**Sample Agenda**

*Objective:* To make strong closers of the salesmen.
1st subject .... 3 minutes.    Recent sales trends showing a need for closing more sales.
2nd subject ___ 3 minutes.    The steps in a sale—attention, interest, desire, action.

# HOW TO PLAN YOUR SALES MEETINGS

3rd subject ___ 16 minutes.  Step number 4—how to close, or how to prompt action.

4th subject ___ 15 minutes.  A movie or some demonstrations on trial closes.

5th subject ___ 3 minutes.  Summary, plea for application in the field, inspirational close.

In the foregoing sample agenda, note the logical sequence of subject matter. The need or reason for strong closing is developed before emphasis is placed on the subject. This makes the salesmen *want* to learn more about closing techniques.

Then the steps in a sale are briefly covered. This shows the relationship of the close to the other steps, pointing up its importance. Thereafter, all emphasis is on the close itself.

### HOW TO DECIDE UPON THE LENGTH OF YOUR MEETING

The length of the meeting should be governed by your objective, because the meeting must last long enough for the objective to be reached. If you cannot accomplish your purpose, something must be changed. You need either a longer meeting or a smaller objective. In such cases, the fault usually is in the objective. Settle for an objective you know you can reach.

An inspirational meeting might be quite short. You can inspire a group in only ten minutes, with a good pep talk.

An instructional type meeting would ordinarily last longer. Instruction should be retained by the audience and it takes time to drive information to the retention point. For instance, it's often advisable to present the information visually as well as verbally, or twice instead of once.

A training meeting is still longer, as it involves trial performance. The salesmen "tryout," under supervision during the meeting. Proper habits and techniques are developed. All this takes time.

Your meeting may include some of all of these—inspiration, instruction, and training. In such cases, simply allow more time for the instructional part, and more time still for the section on training. The length of the sections can then be totaled to determine the length of the overall meeting.

Should salesmen be brought in from great distances, longer

meetings are appropriate. Their travel is costly. Having already invested in their travel, you'll want a maximum return for your investment. So travel expense is another factor to consider when deciding on the length of the meeting.

Sometimes you'll complete a meeting ahead of schedule. If you're sure the objective of the meeting has been met, call a halt! Stalling for time in order to "run out the clock" is a waste of valuable manpower. Further, it precludes ending the meeting on a high note.

### HOW TO SELECT THE BEST TIME FOR YOUR MEETINGS

Internal factors, such as customer traffic, often have a bearing on the time for your meeting. However, a short meeting can be held nearly any time. A long meeting should be scheduled for a period of the day that is not ordinarily productive.

Early morning meetings are best because people are more alert and receptive at that time of day. Also, this enables the salesmen to plunge into their work immediately—before enthusiasm has worn off. Evening meetings, on the other hand, may send everyone home to sleep off his enthusiasm.

The same principle is observed in selecting the day of the week. The early part ordinarily is better. Meetings at the end of the week may generate fire at the time it is least productive.

### HOW TO CHOOSE THE PERSONNEL TO ATTEND YOUR MEETING

"People attending a meeting should have common needs and interests," states an Oklahoma sales executive. "This enables you to present subject matter that is applicable to all. A clerk in the accounting department doesn't need information on sales techniques, nor is he interested in it. 'Birds of a feather' should be flocked together. Then your sales meetings will show results."

Of course, general information is more universal in its application. Such subjects as sick leave policy and payroll deductions can profitably be presented to employees whose jobs are quite different, as well as to experienced, and inexperienced salesmen. But information on how to use new cash registers would apply only to cashiers. Rules regarding expense accounts would concern only those who travel. For such specific information, the audience should be narrowed to the people concerned.

The type of meeting helps determine the size of the audience. For instance, a training meeting ordinarily includes a "tryout" by every person attending. This indicates that training sessions can best be conducted for small audiences.

Some meetings include group discussion. In such instances, a small audience is best. Group discussion is not sufficiently dynamic to keep the interest of a large crowd.

An inspirational meeting, on the contrary, can be conducted for a large audience. The size of the crowd tends in itself to be inspirational.

**PLAN A POSITIVE TONE FOR YOUR MEETING**

Sales meetings have not always been enjoyable. As a gruff old timer explained it, "I called my employees together every week whether I had anything to say or not. It kept them on their toes-let them know I was the boss. Besides, there was always something to jump on them about."

Since sales can always be higher, salespeople caught the brunt of it. Even when other personnel were excluded, salespeople were often made to suffer through such meetings.

But the boss finally realized that his tactics were wrong. As American business grew up, the boss grew up with it. He learned that good sales meetings are conducted on a positive plane, that salespeople must be encouraged rather than reprimanded. He found that emphasis should be placed on the successes of today and the plans for tomorrow—not on yesterday's failures.

A supervisor may be extremely dissatisfied with his salesmen. Even so, there's little to be gained from "reading the riot act" to them. An open admission that things are all wrong is an admission that management may also be at fault. It usually causes a group of salesmen to defend themselves and, if possible, to strike back.

Good planning, therefore, sometimes includes restraint. Mistakes are covered with sufficient tact. An error is referred to as possibly an isolated instance. The meeting is then better received.

### A Case in Point

Here's a case history—An appliance manufacturer developed a "canned" sales presentation. It worked very well. But the salesmen didn't continue using it. They became "too smart" to use it. They added things, omitted others. Before long there was little resemblance between how they were selling and how they *should* have been selling. Result: sales dropped sharply. When the sales manager discovered the trouble, he hit the roof! "Those idiots! I ought to fire every one of them! I'll really tell them a thing or two!"

Did he? Of course not. He was too intelligent for that. Instead, he planned a sales meeting in a positive vein. The meeting covered:

- .... Why a "canned" presentation was developed.
- .... How it was developed
- ... The expense incurred in development
- .... Proof of its success, including several examples.
- .... How to use the presentation
- .... Demonstrations of its use
- .... An appeal for its use in the field.
- .... The announcement that several of the staff would be asked to report their success with it at the next meeting.

As might be expected, reaction to the meeting was quite favorable. Instead of being bawled out, the men were sold on the idea of using the presentation, shown how to use it, and were inspired to follow through. Sales volume started climbing immediately.

The point: a sales meeting is not a place to blow-off steam. Good meetings are usually based on a positive tone.

### HOW TO PLAN YOUR SALES MEETINGS

Determine the Objective of Your Meeting

Give Your Audience What It Wants

Prepare an Agenda Based on Your Objective

# HOW TO PLAN YOUR SALES MEETINGS

**Decide Upon the Length of Your Meeting**

**Select the Best Time for Your Meeting**

**Choose the Proper Personnel to Attend**

**Plan a Positive Tone for Your Meeting**

# 3. How to Build Your Meetings Around a Central Theme

Once a meeting has been planned, the big job is in getting the salesmen to listen! People aren't good listeners as they once were. Employees, particularly salespeople, no longer sit in awe and respect while company officials talk for hours on end. The modern salesperson has a greater feeling of independence. He's attentive as long as the meeting is so interesting that it commands or deserves his attention.

**USE DEMONSTRATION, NOT CONVERSATION**

The day of dry speeches is over. Salespeople want to be shown. They want demonstration, not conversation. So why base a meeting on speeches? Everyone wants action—something to see or do. Showmanship in sales meetings is now essential!

### Build Your Meeting Around a Central Theme

A central theme is good showmanship. If well projected, the theme puts life in a meeting, helps keep the attention and interest of the audience.

A Long Beach retailer declared, "Our meetings are much better received now that we're using central themes. Each meeting has more overall significance and meaning. And the theme helps connect each event within a meeting. It provides continuity."

# BUILD MEETINGS AROUND A CENTRAL THEME

### HOW TO SELECT AN APPROPRIATE THEME

There's no limit to the number of ideas around which a theme can be built. But before selecting a theme, review your agenda. Then decide which theme will help most in dramatizing your agenda.

Themes are somewhat flexible. But be sure the theme selected is in accord with the objective of the meeting. The theme should actually help accomplish your objective.

For example, if your objective is to get salesmen to make more calls, the "Back To School" theme is not appropriate. The words, "Back To School" imply training rather than motivation. Themes such as "Go Getter" or "Big Game Hunt" would be better. The "Go Getter" theme is centered on the idea of making every salesman a "Go Getter." The "Big Game Hunt" is based upon searching for some big customers or big sales.

Also, you should consider the theme's appeal to your particular type of sales organization. Two-fisted salesmen at the wholesale level would sneer at a Valentine theme. However, it would be acceptable to a group of ladies who sell cosmetics direct to the consumer.

Themes of interest and benefit to new men may be boring to salesmen with more experience. This, too, should be considered. Some firms conduct separate meetings for new men.

### HOW TO APPLY YOUR CENTRAL THEME

Now apply the theme to your agenda. Go over each event, tying in the many ideas suggested by the theme. A little imagination pays big dividends.

At a small meeting, strong tie-in of the theme can appear to be juvenile. But at larger meetings, there's room for color. And if ladies are present, the audience is even more receptive to stunts relating to the theme.

For example, a sales meeting conducted for 10 or 15 men should not receive strong application of the theme. Why put on a show without an audience? With a group of 200 or more, however, emphasis on the theme should be heavy.

# 18 *BUILD MEETINGS* AROUND A *CENTRAL THEME*

The following outlines were successfully used by some of the largest corporations in the country. They show how ordinary sales meetings, completely lacking in luster, can be made colorful, interesting and enjoyable.

**THEME-ROUNDUP**

Type of Selling—Jobbing or Wholesale

| Agenda Before Applying Theme | Agenda After Applying Theme |
|---|---|
| Start with talk on why we need more customers. | Play recorded western music, something peppy, for five minutes prior to meeting while group is gathering. |
| Second speaker talks on how to get more customers. | |
| Third speaker talks on how to keep customers. | Emcee, dressed as cowboy, introduces roundup theme before presenting the first speaker. |
| Sales Manager closes meeting with pep talk. | "The Big Roundup" is title for speaker wearing ten-gallon hat who tells why we should "round up" more customers. |
| | "How To Lasso New Customers" is subject for speaker wearing a bandana who tells how to make a sales presentation. At end of talk he throws lasso around "customer" to dramatize successful completion of sale. |
| | Rustler Skit—A competitor is caught trying to steal a customer. |
| | "Keep 'em Corralled" will be covered by speaker wearing a tin badge and six shooter who tells what he does to "keep 'em in the herd"—how to "brand" a customer for life. |
| | "Open Range" is topic for Sales Manager, who closes meeting |

# BUILD MEETINGS AROUND A CENTRAL THEME 19

with inspirational talk on the abundance of prospects, urging salesmen to be "top hands" or first rate "range bosses" by thoroughly developing their territories.

**THEME-APRIL SHOWERS**

Type of Selling—Over the Counter

| Agenda Before Applying *Theme* | *Agenda* After Applying *Theme* |
|---|---|
| Start with talk on why and how to be courteous to customers. | A record of the tune "April Showers" is played while group is gathering. |
| Second speaker talks on product information—why the salespeople must have product knowledge and how to get more product knowledge. | Emcee, holding an open umbrella over his head, introduces theme, "April Showers." |
| Third speaker covers suggestion selling and trading up. | Speaker wearing slicker tells why and how to be courteous to customers. He ties in theme with expressions such as, "Shower the customer with attention and service." |
| Merchandise Manager makes inspirational talk. | Speaker wearing trench coat makes product information talk. Points out that rainy days reduce customer traffic, thus are good for studying products and manufacturers' literature. |
| | Speaker covering suggestion selling and trading up uses examples involving rainy day merchandise—door mats, galoshes, and so forth. |
| | Merchandise Manager's talk includes references to the theme, such as, "Everyone makes a habit of getting out of the rain. Let's |

# 20    BUILD MEETINGS AROUND A CENTRAL THEME

also make a habit of customer courtesy, complete product knowledge, suggestion selling and trading up."

Stage money is taped to the ceiling before the meeting, affixed in such a way that a pull on a string near the speakers' stand, releases the many bogus bills. The meeting is climaxed and concluded when the emcee states that everyone who applies the principles of the meeting will be showered with money. Emcee then yells, "April Showers," and pulls the string, showering the audience with stage money.

### THEME-SALES FEVER

Type of Selling—Any Type

| Agenda *Before* Applying Theme | Agenda After Applying Theme |
|---|---|
| Start with talk on attitude and willingness to work. | Place large poster, on which a thermometer has been drawn behind the speakers' stand. |
| Second speaker explains how to get more sales. | Emcee, dressed as a doctor and with stethoscope around neck, introduces theme—Sales Fever, a burning desire to make more sales. |
| Third speaker speaks about positive thinking. | |
| Recognition of top producers. | |
| Inspirational talk. | "My First Symptoms" is title of the talk. Working overtime willingly, thinking about how to do a better job while off duty and, going the extra mile to get a sale, are stressed. |
| | "I Broke Into A Rash"—a rash of new customers. Speaker tells how he obtained the customers. |

# BUILD MEETINGS AROUND A CENTRAL THEME        21

"Suddenly Stricken"—Salesman in audience starts moaning as if suddenly stricken ill. Someone in nurse's uniform helps him to speakers' stand, where emcee (in doctor's garb) briefly examines him. Condition diagnosed as Sales Fever. Treatment: given an order book and told to start selling.

"My Headache" is title of talk on why and how to think positively. Head so full of positive thoughts it almost aches!

"Those Who Have The Fever"—outstanding producers are recognized.

"What Sales Fever Did To Me" is title of wind-up talk. It gave speaker a high temperature, a swelling of the pocketbook but, above all, enthusiasm. Talk covers why and how to get Sales Fever or enthusiasm.

As shown by the foregoing examples, it's easy to build your meeting around a theme. Simply outline your agenda, select a theme and apply it. A drab and uninteresting meeting suddenly becomes alive. It now has impact and meaning. Those attending will stay awake, will learn more, will be more inspired, and will welcome the next meeting.

### 52 THEMES YOU CAN USE

| | |
|---|---|
| New Year ........................ | Set goals for the new year. |
| Washington's Birthday .. | Never lie to a customer. |
| Valentine ...................... | Fall in love with your prospect. |
| March Winds ................. | A big blow won't necessarily get the order. |
| April Showers ................ | Shower each customer with service. |
| Easter or New Growth .. | A chance for a new start. |
| Green Thumb ................. | Cultivate new customers. |

## 22  BUILD MEETINGS AROUND A CENTRAL THEME

| | |
|---|---|
| Spring Fling | Wake up and live! |
| Baseball | Hit home runs with your prospects. |
| May Day | Calls for a celebration |
| Decoration Day | Salesmen—the infantry of American business. |
| Graduation | Training series now over. |
| June Bride | Marry your customer. |
| July 4th | Be hot as a firecracker. |
| Summertime | Shirt sleeve session. |
| Vacation | Work now—retire later. |
| Fishing | Fish for the big ones. |
| Back to School | Start of training series. |
| Football or Kickoff | Beginning of new program. |
| Columbus Day | Astounding discovery. |
| Halloween | Spooks are laziness, neglect, et al. |
| Golden Harvest | Commissions to be reaped. |
| Horn of Plenty | Money for everybody. |
| Thanksgiving | Management thanks salesmen. |
| Winter or Winter Whirl | Build a hot fire. |
| Christmas | Gifts for salesmen. |
| Prospecting | Look for customers. |
| Go Getter | Take action. |
| Opportunity | Make the most of it. |
| Treasure Hunt | Let's find it. |
| Pirate | Don't let competitors in. |
| Enthusiasm | go, Go, *GO!* |
| Gold Rush | Get your share. |
| Big Game Hunt | Find the big sales. |
| Pioneers' Party | Be among the first. |
| Black Magic | Calls pay off like magic. |
| Wheel of Fortune | You can make a fortune. |
| Carnival | Don't be a pitch man. |
| Circus or Big Top | Ringmaster, clown, thin man. |
| Masquerade | Prospects wear different disguises. |
| Vaudeville | Have a variety of talents. |
| Cowboy | Roundup customers. |
| Indian or Pow Wow | How. |
| Bury The Hatchet | Regain lost customers. |
| Fiesta | Celebrate over the Latin market. |
| Sell-a-bration | A sales rally. |
| Bonanza | A real gold strike. |
| Road to Success | Take it. Go! |
| Transportation | Let work be your vehicle. |

## BUILD MEETINGS AROUND A CENTRAL THEME 23

Aviation............................ Let's fly high.
Atomic Energy ................ A huge sales explosion.
Courtroom....................... Trial for poor sales practices.

### HAVE SPEAKERS USE THE LANGUAGE OF YOUR THEME

Ask participants to use the language of your theme. Let's assume you're using the Football or Kickoff theme. You could suggest such terms as:

>"Know the rules of the game."
>
>"Call the right signals."
>
>"Take the ball and run with it." "Be a quarterback—not a drawback."

### PLAN DECORATIONS THAT COINCIDE WITH YOUR THEME

Use decorations that coincide with your theme. No need to decorate for a ten minute "quickie" involving a handful of people. But the bigger and longer meetings deserve colorful decorations.

For the Indian or Cowboy theme, decorations might include:

>A wigwam.
>A cigar store Indian.
>Tomahawks.
>War drums.
>Peace pipes.
>Signs saying, "How," "Ugh," and so forth.
>Pictures of Indians or of massacre scenes.

### ARRANGE ENTERTAINMENT THAT FITS YOUR THEME

There's need for entertainment at some sales meetings. The longer and larger meetings especially need a little gayety.

Entertainment should fit the theme. This adds to the impact of the theme, makes it more meaningful.

For the Indian theme, stage an Indian war dance. When using Black Magic as a theme, engage a magician to perform. Or get a juggling act to support the Vaudeville theme. Conduct a bingo game with the Carnival theme.

# 24  BUILD MEETINGS AROUND A CENTRAL THEME

## SERVE REFRESHMENTS THAT PROJECT YOUR THEME

Some sales meetings are so lengthy that refreshments are served. Here's another chance to project your theme.

Turkey sandwiches, pumpkin pie, and coffee fit the Thanksgiving theme. For the Prospecting theme, serve cookies molded in the shape of burros, shovels, and picks. The Circus theme can be expressed with popcorn, peanuts, and soda pop.

"Anyone can serve coffee every time," said an imaginative New Englander. "Give 'em something different, something that fits the theme of your meeting."

## USE ANNOUNCEMENTS THAT CARRY OUT YOUR THEME

Even the announcements of your meeting should reflect your theme.

Take the Harvest theme, for instance. A verbal announcement could include: "We'll show you how to sow the seeds of greater profit, how to get a larger yield, how to reap a bumper crop of customers." A written announcement might contain pictures of a farmer, barn, plow, tractor, and silo.

Announcement forms or bulletin heads can be obtained from a number of commercial houses. They contain headings that have been copyrighted. You can print or mimeograph your own message underneath the heading.

For instance, most of the 52 themes previously listed can be found on these announcement forms. The bulletins depicting the New Year's theme may show an old man, a scythe, an hour glass, and a baby. The heading sets the stage for your copy.

You can order such bulletin heads in any quantities you desire, they save you some art work and simplify your job. These bulletin heads can be obtained in color, and are quite attractive.

To find out where bulletin heads can be obtained, inquire of the president of your nearest Sales Executives Club.

## HOW TO BUILD YOUR MEETINGS AROUND A CENTRAL THEME

Select a Theme That's Compatible With Your Objective Be Sure the Theme Fits Your Type of Organization

# *BUILD MEETINGS AROUND A CENTRAL THEME*

Apply the Theme to Your Agenda

Work Your Theme Into Every Event Possible

Ask Participants to Use Language of Your Theme

Use Decorations That Coincide With Your Theme

Plan Entertainment That Fits Your Theme

Serve Refreshments That Project Your Theme

Use Announcements That Reflect Your Theme

# 4.  How to Use Variety and Showmanship

It may surprise you to learn that you are compared with Frank Sinatra and Perry Como. Perhaps you don't claim to be a singer. None the less, you're compared with these and other singing stars, including Patti Page and Dinah Shore.

You may not consider yourself an actor. Yet people compare you with Marlon Brando and Spencer Tracy. You are continually compared with the top names in show business even though you're not an entertainer. Here's why . . .

Whether John Q. American is "out of town" or is withdrawn to the privacy of his living room, he can see professionally staged programs. Even in the intimacy of his bedroom, he can enjoy radio and television.

Such entertainment is supported by multi-million dollar networks. It's the product of experienced writers, producers, directors, technicians, prop men, make-up artists, and others. Thousands of dollars are spent on piddling details. Everything is carefully worked out. Perfection is more than an aim—it's an obsession.

**SALESPEOPLE DEMAND THE BEST**

The result of all this has been a loss of tolerance. People have become less and less tolerant of a mediocre production. They want the best and expect to get it. And, what's more, they expect the best in all types of programming—even sales meetings!

Audiences have been conditioned—not to a slow pace set by

# HOW *TO USE* VARIETY AND *SHOWMANSHIP* 27

a succession of boring speeches. They are accustomed to a lively pace, a good selection of subject matter, skilled dramatizations, proper timing, a refreshing variety of events, and the many other elements of good showmanship. Since they get good showmanship elsewhere, they understandably frown on a sales meeting in which it is lacking.

What a challenge! A sales executive should be such a good showman that his stage presence compares favorably with people of the entertainment profession. He should have timing, color, humor, change of pace, adroitness, resourcefulness, tact, urbanity, and sensitivity. Showmanship is a prime requisite. It's the difference between a meeting and a *good* meeting.

You can meet this challenge, in part, by building your meetings around a central theme. Also, you can be dramatic, bizarre. You can do the unusual. But an additional step toward meeting the challenge is to stage a variety of events.

### A Good Showman Uses Variety

You should have many different things on the agenda so there'll be changes of pace. Take a page from the book of the circus ringmaster, who surprises his audience time after time by presenting the unexpected.

There are many ways of creating a change of pace. Catalogue the areas to be considered, including specific techniques of staging. Before each meeting, check your agenda against these many methods of adding variety.

#### ROTATE CHAIRMANSHIP OF THE MEETINGS TO CREATE VARIETY

Variety can be created by rotating the responsibility for meetings among assistants and the strongest salespeople. Each takes a turn at planning and staging a meeting.

Most of us have a false sense of pride, the feeling that no one else can do the job as well as we can. But an accomplished executive delegates responsibility to others; he personally does little more than supervise.

# 28  HOW *TO USE* VARIETY AND *SHOWMANSHIP*

A top flight sales executive can walk out of many of his meetings the moment they begin—and with no harm done. When all goes well, he can be proud of his organizational ability. By letting others play a major role, he takes a load off his own shoulders and helps develop the people under him.

The main point here, however, is that *it* gives *variety to the meeting.* Each get-together has a different personality and a different viewpoint behind it. This keeps the series of meetings fresh and crisp.

Most sales forces consist primarily of men—many solely of men. Where there are a few women, though, the sales-manager could let them run an entire meeting, calling it Ladies Day. Or if the organization is headed by a woman and consists primarily of salesladies, the men could be given a chance to show their stuff.

Anything that's a switch from the ordinary will produce some much needed variety.

In certain instances, other departments could stage the meeting. They could show what they do to design, test, produce, ship, or account for the product. This would cause the sales staff to have a better understanding of the overall operation. It would also promote teamwork between the sales department and others.

Still another idea of this type—firms supplying services, materials or products could assume responsibility for a meeting or some part thereof. Suppliers are usually well-versed on their own merchandise.

**HOW TO USE A SEMINAR TO VARY THE ROUTINE**

Regardless of who conducts the meeting, the thing to guard against is talk after talk after talk. At least a part of every program should be based on something other than speeches.

The seminar method is a good example of how to vary the routine. One salesman presents a problem with which he has been confronted. Others then attempt to solve that problem. The difficulty involved might be a tough prospect, an unusual selling situation, or a hidden objective. Although he's the last to realize it, the salesman himself might be the problem. Perhaps he's not

# HOW TO USE VARIETY AND SHOWMANSHIP

making enough calls. Or he may not be giving adequate service to old customers. Such weaknesses can often be discovered. Whatever the problem, profitable suggestions are usually forthcoming from the audience.

In addition, a seminar is refreshing because it is a departure from the ordinary.

### HOW TO USE A PANEL DISCUSSION

A panel discussion is also a departure. Four or five qualified people are appointed to the panel and take seats at a table facing the audience. A moderator stands in the center of the panel members. The moderator is not seated since he can better control the situation when standing. He calls on panel members to answer questions. Management can prepare the questions in advance, listing those that will provoke answers and information most needed by the audience.

It is often better, on the other hand, to use questions originated by the audience, as this assures coverage of material in which there is the greatest interest. Where questions come from the audience, they should be submitted in advance in written form. This provides opportunity to screen them, eliminating those that are objectionable. They need not be submitted days in advance—at the start of the meeting should be early enough, because it will take only a few minutes to decide which ones are irrelevant, too negative, or will be answered by speeches slated to follow. Another reason for screening is to eliminate duplication.

"I thought I was smart enough to handle questions without screening," said a corporation board member. "But it got me into hot water right away. Don't try it. Take the few minutes that are necessary for screening."

As for accepting verbal questions from the floor, only in small meetings is this recommended. It's justified in small meetings since it results in a fair degree of audience participation. But it's risky business unless the moderator is skilled, because he must be able to recognize objectionable questions and to brush them off in a manner that does not offend. "This isn't easy either," said a Baton Rouge sales manager. "People are inclined to wear their feelings on their sleeves. One must be very careful—more careful than he might think."

The moderator gets participation from all members of the panel by limiting each answer to a couple of minutes. But he must know what to do if a member gives an incorrect answer or leaves an erroneous impression.

It's important that one or two members of the audience do not hog the show with their questions. There have been post-meeting comments such as, "If only someone had strangled that character in the third row! Without him, the meeting wouldn't have been so bad."

A rule of thumb: when one member of the audience has spoken a second time, the moderator should thereafter concentrate on getting questions from people who have not previously participated.

Other points of consideration are whether table "mikes" will be needed and whether name cards should be placed on the table in front of panel members. These two items can add much to the event. If name cards are used, however, the printing should be large enough that it can be read by people in the rear of the room.

**HOW TO USE EXPERTS IN AN UNUSUAL WAY**

Another refreshing approach is called The Big Switch. This is where the audience is divided into several groups and an "expert" assigned to each group. The "expert" leads a discussion on pertinent subjects, answering any questions asked of him.

After the "expert" has shared his knowledge for a designated length of time, a whistle is blown. At this signal the "experts" change places. They rotate from group to group until each has spent time with every group.

"We've used this at several meetings," reported a steel company sales official. "It worked well every time. Everybody likes a change from the ordinary.

"Besides," he continued, "I've noticed that the salesmen are glad to get better acquainted with the 'experts.' They take pride in quoting the 'experts/ as if they're close personal friends."

# HOW TO USE VARIETY AND SHOWMANSHIP

This event is especially effective where the audience does not ordinarily have access to the "experts," or to their information and knowledge.

### HOW TO USE DISCUSSION GROUPS

Here's another way of doing it—the areas of major interest are determined. To illustrate, let's assume that the salespeople are interested in four different subjects—the approach, the presentation, objections, and closes. In this event, several chairs are placed in each corner of the room. A key person is designated, one who excels in the subject concerned, to handle each topic. Persons desiring information on a particular subject then meet with the group discussing it; everyone joins the discussion group of his choice.

This arrangement is a workshop in its simplest form. It's effective because there's freedom of decision on the part of the audience and because each salesman receives help in the area where, presumably, he needs it most. Then, too, it's a departure from nothing but speeches.

### HOW TO USE INTERPRETERS

A staff of interpreters will provide a change of pace. At the same time, it gets several people "into the act."

To use this idea, four or five persons are asked to sit at a table near the front of the room. They listen to the next speaker (as does the audience) and then interpret the speech to the audience. They give their analyses, their opinions regarding key points, and their summations of the talk. This helps drive home the main points in the speech. Thus, while it's good showmanship, it's also sound instruction. By using a different staff of interpreters for each talk, even more variety is created.

### HOW TO STAGE THE COURTROOM PLAN

Have you tried the courtroom procedure? There are different ways of using the courtroom plan, but the format is always the same. The basic idea is that something or someone is on trial.

## 32 HOW *TO USE* VARIETY AND *SHOWMANSHIP*

*A* successful salesman is "tried" for poor selling practices. Although he is found to be "not guilty/' the questioning which leads to the verdict reveals some excellent sales practices. The audience is more receptive when the information is brought out in this manner instead of through lecture.

To show the wrong way of doing a job, or the pitfalls to be avoided, the salesman is found "guilty" of certain undesirable practices.

The courtroom procedure is also good for introducing a new sales tool or merchandising aid. Several "witnesses" testify regarding the need for a certain sales aid. Others then testify regarding the new tool that fills that particular need. They explain how the new tool should be used, they demonstrate it, and they urge others to employ it immediately. Even a new product can be introduced in this manner and to make a real production out of it, there can be a "judge" who swears in a dozen people as the "jury," seating them apart from the rest of the audience. A "defense counsel" is appointed. By prearrangement he adds color to the questioning of "witnesses" by objecting several times!

**HOW TO MAKE USE OF THE COMPETITIVE INSTINCT**

Most people like to see how well they can do a thing, especially if competition is involved.

Prior to a meeting, various subjects are written on separate slips of paper. Subjects about which the audience needs more information are the only subjects selected. During the meeting, volunteers are asked to draw a slip. Each reads the subject written on his slip and immediately gives a two minute talk on it.

This results in an unorganized but rapid-fire barrage of useful information. It puts several additional people on the program, which is also desirable. A prize can be given for the best speech.

In the case of large meetings, a more professional atmosphere should prevail. A wheel, such as the type used at carnivals, serves the purpose better than drawing the slips of paper. Instead of numbers, the wheel has subjects printed on it. A person spins the wheel and speaks on the subject indicated.

# HOW *TO USE* VARIETY AND *SHOWMANSHIP*

## HOW TO ADD VARIETY THROUGH COSTUMING

Costuming adds a touch of showmanship. It also produces variety.

This is a fascinating little stunt: before the meeting starts, five or six salesmen are secretly ushered into an adjacent room. Each is given a false face to wear. During the meeting these people are called in, one at a time. Each is said to represent a common objection, such as not interested, price, I'll think it over, and others. Then it is proved that objections are false—"Just as false as the faces being worn."

Methods of answering each objection are given and if the meeting is not too large, the audience can supply the answers. After an objection is answered, the participant is unmasked and the audience told, "See what a fine looking prospect he is? He even smiles! He wasn't really objecting. He merely threw up a false front so you wouldn't consider him a pushover. He wanted you to work for the sale."

In addition to subject matter, the theme of the meeting offers excellent suggestion for costuming.

### OUTSIDE SPEAKERS CAN BE EFFECTIVE

Outside speakers can be used occasionally. An aggressive sales executive from another firm will sometimes work wonders. He probably will tell the group nothing more than they've been hearing, but it's often more effective when they hear it from someone else. An outsider doesn't have an "axe to grind."

There are Sales Executive Clubs in most cities of over 150,000. The Secretary of each Club can usually supply the names of local people who are capable of delivering a bona fide message. To glamorize the event, the visitor could be billed as a mystery guest.

### HOW TO USE A MIND READING ACT

At a sales meeting in Detroit, a participant was introduced as The Great Swami. He had a towel wrapped around his head and was said to be capable of mind reading. A member of the audience was called to the front. The Great Swami supposedly read his mind.

After heavy concentration the Great Swami stated the first thought lifted from the subject's mind: "I hope . . . I hope my wife . . . I hope my wife really thinks I'm going to see a sick friend tonight." Then the second thought: "Our sales manager is . . . Our sales manager is much worse than Simon Legree!"

After a couple of laughs, some constructive "thoughts" were brought out. One was: "I should push the hard-to-sell items instead of being just an order taker for the articles in demand." Another was: "I can fit our merchandise into the customer's needs if I take the trouble to learn what needs actually exist."

**STARTLE THEM WITH A CORONER'S INQUEST**

A sales promotion manager devised a sensational way to introduce a new merchandising aid. He conducted a coroner's inquest!

Several days before the meeting, he showed the new aid to several top salesmen. In the interest of field testing, a few were permitted to use it.

Then came the meeting . . . When the sales promotion manager was introduced there was no mention of his subject. As he rose to speak a recording of a funeral march was played. A mock funeral procession entered from the rear of the room! It was lead by an "undertaker," complete with dark suit and stovepipe hat. Two "pallbearers" followed, carrying a "casket."

When the procession reached the front of the room, the speaker called it to a halt. The music was also stopped, and the emcee asked for an explanation. "We're burying an unsuccessful salesman," explained the "undertaker." When asked the cause of death the "undertaker" replied, "I don't know, but we're burying all of them. Something is putting an end to all the unsuccessful salesmen."

The speaker had the casket placed on a table while a coroner's inquest was conducted. Ten "witnesses" were called to the front and seated apart from the audience. They were questioned one at a time.

# HOW *TO USE* VARIETY AND *SHOWMANSHIP*  35

The first expressed the opinion that unsuccessful salesmen were being eliminated by a new sales aid his department had designed. "It's a tool so powerful that no salesman will hereafter be unsuccessful." Other witnesses confirmed the opinion. Salesmen who had field tested the item told of their success in using it. By carefully selecting the "witnesses" and asking well prepared questions, the speaker had a very rosy picture painted.

A gavel was banged and the verdict announced: "The findings are that death was caused by the new sales aid. This new aid is bringing an end to all unsuccessful sales efforts." At that moment the "corpse" jumped out of the "casket!" It was a real shocker since the audience had no reason to believe someone was actually in the box! He ran to the speakers' stand and grabbed the new sales aid. Then he raced out of the room yelling, "Don't bury me—I want to use it too!"

This event lasted only 22 minutes. It did ten times as much good as a speech of the same duration. Try it!

**CONSIDER THE OCCASIONAL USE OF ENTERTAINMENT**

Where a light touch is needed, outside entertainers can be used to good advantage. Whether it's a short juggling act or a pretty girl who sings a song, there's a time and place for entertainment. On occasion, a sales meeting is an appropriate time and place.

The size of the audience is one of the determining factors. The theme, length, and objective of the meeting should also be considered. Prime consideration, however, is the need for showmanship.

**CONDUCT INTERVIEWS WITH MEMBERS OF THE AUDIENCE**

As you can see, there are many ways to toss a change-up. So there's no reason for a program to be loaded with one boring talk after another. Relief from the usual series of talks can be realized in hundreds of ways.

Members of the audience are called to the speakers' stand for

## 36  HOW *TO USE VARIETY* AND *SHOWMANSHIP*

brief interviews. Or the emcee walks into the audience, possibly with a portable mike, to conduct interviews which brings about audience participation, and is much to be desired. More important—it varies the routine.

**PROVIDE A GOAL AT WHICH TO SHOOT**

Every salesperson does better when he has a goal. After all, how can he hit the bull's eye unless he has a target at which to shoot? Since goals spur salesmen on to greater accomplishments, sales meetings have often been based on goals.

For example, an enterprising sales supervisor arranged an unusual but successful meeting . . . When people entered the meeting room they were surprised to find a beautiful new automobile on display. They found a flashy speedboat, pictures of a lovely new home, a chic model wearing a mink stole, and several other attractions. Each item was tagged so that persons viewing it could tell what had to be done to earn it. These were not prizes, but were suggested goals. During the meeting the value of goals was discussed, and all present were urged to set goals for themselves.

The idea paid off handsomely. It caused increased effort on the part of nearly everyone on the sales staff! It also put showmanship in the meeting, causing it to be anything but run-of-the-mill. Incidentally, when arranging a meeting of this type you can probably borrow the merchandise from local merchants.

A variation of the foregoing plan has been used in connection with Christmas. Suitable merchandise was displayed in the meeting room. Items included toasters and roasters, as well as luxury items, including jewelry, watches, and luggage. The meeting was conducted in November. The articles of merchandise were suggested as short range goals—Christmas presents.

The audience was told how many extra sales would finance the purchase of each item. Most salesmen wanted Christmas presents for their families and worked hard to earn the articles desired.

Of course, the merchandise could have been offered as prizes,

# HOW TO USE VARIETY AND SHOWMANSHIP

but the details are not our concern here. The objective of this section is to show how to put variety in sales meetings.

## QUIZ PROGRAMS GET POINTS ACROSS

Progressive sales executives sometimes season their meetings with quiz programs. While there are many different ways of conducting such events, here's a "for instance" or two:

Most salespeople are extroverted. They do not enjoy reading sales manuals or dissertations on company policy. It's therefore necessary, from time to time, to stimulate their study of company literature. This can easily be accomplished by a quiz program.

Before the meeting, significant sentences are selected from various pieces of literature. Only the more important points are chosen, the things every salesman should know. At the meeting, each man is issued a set of company literature. Then the preselected sentences are read by the emcee. As each sentence is read, the first person to find it in the literature wins a point toward the prize. He jumps up and shouts the title of the publication containing it, as well as the number of the page on which it can be found.

The person who wins the most points is awarded a prize. But here's the real payoff—after each sentence is found in the literature, someone is asked to explain it. He enlarges on it, applies it to the salesman's job. This results in a better understanding of procedures and policies. Product information can also be learned in this manner.

Sales trainers have found written tests a good means of lending variety. True-false tests are most popular, although multiple choice and completion type tests are also used. Every salesman grades his own paper. The grade is actually of little importance; the underlying teaching point is the significant thing. In a discussion following each point, the trainer brings out the why and wherefore, letting everyone know what he's expected to do as a result. Still other quiz programs have been patterned after those seen on television. It's not difficult to work up an event of this sort, one that is profitable, yet enjoyable. Give it a try.

# 38 HOW *TO* USE VARIETY AND *SHOWMANSHIP*

HOW TO USE CONTESTS TO SPICE YOUR MEETINGS

Contests will change the tempo. One side of the room is pitted against the other, or the new men against those with more experience.

Another in-meeting contest is the quiz down, similar to the old fashioned spelling bee. Persons missing a question are eliminated, and the last remaining contestant is the winner. This event is made to move rapidly. It's desirable to increase the pace as people are eliminated, otherwise, the majority will be spectators too much of the time.

A steak and bean dinner has served as a good means of varying the pitch. It's usually based on a sales contest that takes place outside the meeting. The sales staff is divided into two groups. The winning team is served steak at a dinner meeting which climaxes the contest. Members of the losing team, on the other hand, must eat beans. They're served bean soup, bean salad, baked beans as an entree, and jelly beans for dessert!

But there's nothing to be gained from bloating half the sales force, if not demoralizing it. Some of the most productive salesmen will be on the losing team. These individuals will have lost through no fault of their own. Therefore, when the winners have been served steak and the losers are resigned to their fate, steak should be brought in for the losers, too.

**HOW TO USE THE ELEMENT OF SUSPENSE**

For meetings lasting a day or longer, the element of suspense can work wonders. There are several ways to rig up a candle so that it will dramatically trigger some type of action. It could eventually burn down to a fuse, in this manner setting off an explosive. Or it could burn down to a string, finally severing the string with its tiny flame. The triggering action should cause something important to happen, or at least be the signal for something important. It could signal the unveiling of a new product or the naming of a contest winner. The candle is lit at the start of the meeting. Everyone is asked to estimate the exact time the triggering action will take place. An appropriate reward is offered for

# HOW *TO USE* VARIETY AND SHOWMANSHIP 39

the best guess. This helps create interest and suspense. To capitalize fully on the stunt, call attention to the candle at intervals during the meeting.

And those who like things cold instead of hot can forego all this hullabaloo with a candle, and accomplish the same thing with a block of ice. The name of a contest winner is written on a slip of paper, placed in a waterproof envelope, and frozen in the center of a large block of ice. Or a new product makes its initial appearance in this way, having been frozen inside a block of ice.

An important new sales tool, details of a new merchandising plan, or the outline of a new advertising campaign are other items that might be dramatized either with a candle or a block of ice.

### PLANNED INTERRUPTIONS PRODUCE A CHANGE OF PACE

Planned interruptions add zest to the staging of a program. Instead of every new participant being introduced, one of them "interrupts" by approaching the speakers' stand at the proper moment. He barges in with a wise crack or two. Before making his presentation, he is finally introduced. A planned interruption is even more surprising when someone in the audience interrupts the proceedings. Questions are often planted among members of the audience. Planted questions are nothing more than planned interruptions.

Then there's the telephone, which can be located near the speakers' stand and rigged to ring at a certain time. Not only does the interruption by ringing give a different flavor, but the ensuing one-way telephone conversation can be quite meaningful. It can start the introduction of the next speaker or the next subject. It can serve as a call from an important person who could not attend the meeting. It can represent a complaining customer, or help clinch a major point.

### HOW TO USE SKITS TO KEEP INTEREST

Skits can be an effective means of keeping interest. The best skits are the short ones—only a minute or two in length. Through the use of skits some valuable lessons can be put across in a way

# 40 HOW TO USE VARIETY AND SHOWMANSHIP

that will be remembered. Here are some skits that have been successfully put on at various meetings. They are effective because they are brief, lively and easily staged. Each of these should spark several ideas for skits of your own.

### SIX SKITS YOU CAN USE

1. At a prearranged time a salesman in the audience starts moaning loud as if suddenly stricken quite ill. Two other sales men rush him to the front of the room and supposedly inject five hundred thousand units of "spizzerinktum" from a five gallon water bottle. Promptly revived, the salesman starts showing enthusiasm. He grabs an order book and rushes out of the room as if to call on prospective customers, following which someone gives a few words on the need for enthusiasm.

2. Any salesman is called to the front and asked to hold his breath as long as he can. The emcee acts as timekeeper. After the time has been announced (usually 20 or 25 seconds), the emcee gives the salesman a goal at which to shoot, adding ten or fifteen seconds to the time of the initial try. The same fellow holds his breath again. Invariably, he will hold it long enough to attain the goal set for him. The moral should then be explained: one always does better when he has a goal.

3. Two members of the audience start arguing in a very realistic manner. They get louder, so the emcee asks them to be quiet. They continue arguing until the emcee asks them to come to the front and explain the disagreement. One gives the opinion that servicing a customer is more important than obtaining the account in the first place. But the other argues that service is of little importance. A show of hands by the audience decides the issue. The point is then further clinched by the emcee's remarks.

4. Someone posing as a newsboy interrupts at an appropriate time, yelling—"Extra, extra! Salesman shot for asking for the order!" The emcee then explains that no such headline has ever been printed, that no such paper will ever be sold. No salesman has ever been shot because he asked for the order. "You won't get

# HOW *TO USE* VARIETY AND *SHOWMANSHIP*

hurt because of it, and you might make more sales. So always ask for the order!"

5. Three people are called to the front and given balloons to blow up. The emcee explains that each balloon represents the individual's opportunity with the company. All blow together to see who can make the most of his opportunity. By prearrangement, one person tries in vain to inflate his balloon. The next inflates his but lets it go. The third inflates his balloon until it bursts.

The emcee then points out that the first person didn't make anything of his opportunity, and that the second person let the opportunity get away from him. "But the third person burst the opportunity wide open. And that's what we want to do-burst this opportunity wide open!"

6. At a suitable time in the program a salesman in the audience hollers—"I want to become a top producer. How can I do it?" The emcee has the man come to the front and stick his head in a bucket of water. The salesman soon needs to breathe and struggles to get his head out. But the emcee holds his head down a few seconds longer to create a real struggle. After the salesman gets his head out, the emcee says, "When you want to be a top producer as badly as you wanted to get your head out of that water, then you'll be a top producer—that's how to do it!"

**BORROW FROM THE THEATER**

The crossover, a technique of the theater, tends to animate a meeting. Signs are carried across the stage, the bearers remaining silent. Each sign contains a major point. As the point is made verbally, it is also made visually.

Another use of such signs is in providing humor. As an example, the point of a speaker's talk might be, "Know your merchandise." At the proper time someone crosses with a sign which states, "Only a goof ..." A few steps behind him there's another person, his sign stating, "Would ever fail ..." Then comes the third person, his sign saying, "To know his merchandise!"

All crossovers are rehearsed to perfect the timing. Persons crossing the stage act casual—even a little indifferent.

# 42 HOW TO USE VARIETY AND *SHOWMANSHIP*

## HOW TO USE GIVEAWAYS EFFECTIVELY

Small giveaways help make one meeting different from the others. At a meeting designed to motivate, those present were given lapel type badges. Printed on each badge was "IRMG-BGOMB." The letters stand for "I'll Reach My Goal By Getting Off My Bottom!"

One firm, putting emphasis on its first advertisement in a national magazine, passed out large lapel buttons containing the words, "I've seen it—have you?"

Any novel idea related to the theme of the meeting might be used as a giveaway. At a meeting based on the Valentine theme, wives and sweethearts were invited and small heart-shaped boxes of candy were distributed. On another occasion, hats that reflected the theme were passed out and donned on the spot.

At a meeting of salesmen who were all being compensated on a commission basis, large wallets were given away. The name of the salesman was engraved on his billfold, making the gift personalized. The wallets were, "For carrying the additional commissions you'll make by applying the information imparted at this meeting."

Another unique giveaway is an unsigned check. A company in Texas offered $50 to every salesman who produced a certain amount of volume within a specified period of time. An unsigned check for the $50 bonus was made in favor of each salesman. The checks were distributed at a meeting. The men kept the checks as constant reminders of the extra "half-hundred" that could be earned. This made the cash offer more meaningful, caused everyone to work harder at earning it.

## HOW TO HIT THE JACKPOT

Some marketing firms do not enjoy an employer-employee relationship with their salespeople. These sales companies must work exceptionally hard at conducting good sales meetings, as attendance can hardly be required when an employer-employee relationship does not exist. The salespeople are independent contractors.

# HOW TO USE VARIETY AND SHOWMANSHIP 43

Because less can be required, attendance at meetings is often low. Further, some of the people attending may not be very productive. Under those conditions, a jackpot drawing can do much toward improving the situation.

As people enter the meeting room, they sign slips of paper which are put in a large bowl. When the meeting begins, a slip is drawn from the bowl and the name is read aloud. The person whose name is drawn must prove he has made at least a minimum number of sales since the previous meeting. If he can do this he receives the jackpot.

This type of drawing is good for several reasons: it helps get people to the meeting, it encourages them to get there on time, it gets them there with a sale or two to their credit, and it adds sparkle to the affair. Perhaps a promptness drawing or some sort of jackpot will give a flair of showmanship to your meetings. Why not try it?

A manufacturing firm featured a bedroom suit as the promptness prize; however, when the prize was given away it proved to be a pair of pajamas!

### LET THEM TELL ABOUT THE BENEFITS

Testimonials help sell sales meetings. Some of the more popular and successful salesmen are asked to give testimonials. They tell exactly what sales meetings have done for them. To pinpoint it, a salesman reports on how he was helped by something presented at the previous meeting or he even tells of benefits received from the meeting presently being conducted.

It's refreshing to the audience to hear such comments from salesmen, because too often they come from company officials. It's a good way to vary the routine.

### HOW TO USE A CORPORATE "CHARACTER"

A novel idea is that of a corporate "character." Several firms have adopted a mannequin, others a dressmaker's dummy. They use the prop again and again. It adds a feeling of realism, as the dummy can be a customer who "listens" to sales presentations and

# 44  HOW *TO USE VARIETY AND SHOWMANSHIP*

"voices" objections. Or he can typify the company salesman, or serve as the symbol of good salesmanship.

Corporate "characters" have been named Sammy Surefire, Georgie Gogetter, and Willie Salesmaker. A producer of mens' hats named his "character" Harry the Hat, while a manufacturer of ladies' skirts selected the moniker Fanny Fullskirt. In some instances corporate "characters" have become as much a part of the organization as the coffee break.

### Variety Is the Spice of Life

As you can see, there are many ways to give a flavor of variety to your meetings. Keep your salesmen guessing. Variety is truly the spice of sales meetings as well as the spice of life.

When more variety is needed, use some of the ideas explained in this chapter. They will spark still other ideas—ideas of your own. Use them. Be a showman. Good showmanship is essential.

### HOW TO USE VARIETY AND SHOWMANSHIP

| | |
|---|---|
| Rotate Chairmanship | Goal Merchandise |
| Seminar | Christmas Presents |
| Panel Discussion | Quiz Programs |
| The Big Switch | Contests |
| Discussion Groups | Steak-Bean Dinner |
| "Interpreters" | Candle or Ice |
| Courtroom Procedure | Interruptions |
| Impromptu Speakers | Skits |
| Costuming | Crossovers |
| Outside Speakers | Giveaways |
| The Great Swami | Jackpot |
| Coroner's Inquest | Promptness Drawing |
| Entertainment | Testimonials |
| Interviews | Corporate "Characters" |

# 5. How to Use Audio-Visual Aids Effectively

In 1939 Hitler was asked to name Germany's most potent weapon of war. Hitler gave a strange but accurate reply. He said, "My most potent weapons are my 60,000 motion picture projectors." And Hitler was right, heavy use of propaganda movies created a fanatic loyalty to the Nazi cause, while liberal use of training films helped shape a well-trained military machine.

The projectors gave Hitler a huge advantage in mass communications, after movie houses and public meeting halls were brought under control. Viewers saw only what it was intended for them to see, and the results are recorded in history. Audio-visual aids proved their value beyond any doubt.

Audio-visual aids have also proved their value in sales meetings. They're splendid for instruction and motivating salesmen. The use of such aids is good showmanship, too, as meetings become more lively when spiced with something extra to see or hear.

**MOVIES AND FILMSTRIPS ARE OFTEN MISUSED**

Except for blackboards, the aids most commonly used in sales meetings are movies and filmstrips. But movies and filmstrips are often misused.

What frequently happens is this: a sales executive hears of a new film, or happens to see it at a meeting outside his company. His natural reaction is to want all his salespeople to see it. So he obtains the film and has it shown to his personnel. He works the meeting into the film instead of working the film into the meeting.

This is wrong. Any visual aid should be used as a means to an end, because the objective of the meeting is the desired end result. The visual aid is only a means of accomplishing that end result, and instead of building a program around a visual aid, you should base the meeting on company and employee needs. Then select the aids that will help most in satisfying those needs.

When properly used, however, visual aids add color and showmanship. They increase the effectiveness of any meeting. They give the presentation a professional touch and make it more acceptable to the audience. Attention and interest are greater. The audience will better understand the material presented and will retain it longer.

**MANY FIRMS PRODUCE THEIR OWN FILMS**

Larger concerns have produced their own movies, filmstrips, and slides. They have aids tailored to their specific needs.

Many companies have produced sales presentations on film. Such films are excellent for training.

Other firms have put their product stories on film. Both salespeople and customers can benefit from this type of visual aid.

Direct selling companies have produced slides for use at the point of sale.

Production costs are dependent on a number of things, but a 16mm sound motion picture can be made for about $1,000 per minute of running time. The cost of extra prints will average about $5 per minute of running time.

A filmstrip is a series of pictures pieced together on one strip of film. It does not produce "movies." Instead, it gives a series of "stills." A phonograph built into the projector is usually used for sound.

The 35mm filmstrips are less expensive to produce, averaging about $500 per minute of running time. Additional prints cost only about 50 cents per minute of running time.

Slides cost even less. Where substantial quantities are used,

# USING AUDIO-VISUAL AIDS EFFECTIVELY

color slides can be produced at an average cost of only 10 cents each. Slides can be made on any subject—product, plant, sales aids, raw materials or personnel.

### WHERE TO FIND THE GREATEST SOURCE OF AUDIO-VISUAL AIDS

The greatest source of visual aids is the commercial film library. Located in all major cities, such agencies are in the business of selling and renting audio-visual aids and will provide whatever you want.

"I've found the commercial film libraries to be quite helpful," stated a Philadelphia man. "If they don't have what you want, they'll get it. That's their business."

Also, many State Universities have film libraries. Their movies and filmstrips cover salesmanship, human relations, and other business subjects. These films are rented to business and industrial concerns at a very nominal charge.

A few major corporations lend films as a public relations gesture, as do some trade associations. Some of these films contain a minimum of advertising and, thus, are quite effective.

You should contact all sources. Become acquainted with the aids available. Then, when planning a meeting, consider the various films. Employ those that are best for reaching your objective.

### TEST YOUR PROJECTION EQUIPMENT BEFOREHAND

Projection equipment should be tested at least several hours before use. By checking things beforehand, you'll have time to order repair work or replacement parts. If the machine cannot readily be fixed, you'll have time to get a substitute.

"I had to learn this the hard way," confessed a chap in Des Moines. "Because the machine worked the last time I used it, I thought it should work the next time. But even if it should, it sometimes didn't. Now I test it beforehand."

As the equipment is set up, electrical cords should be protected so that the power will not be cut off by a careless footstep. The cords can be covered by rugs and run outside the traffic lanes.

Some "play" in the cords will provide for further protection. Also, cords can be taped to the baseboard near the wall outlet, to make a disconnection even less likely.

The screen should be high enough so that persons sitting in the rear of the room can see. This means that the bottom of the screen must be higher than the heads of the people who will sit on the front row. Ordinarily, the *bottom* of the screen must be nearly five feet high.

If a loudspeaker is used it can best be located on a chair or table near the screen. This produces clear and more realistic sound effects. At a signal previously agreed upon, the projectionist can turn on the speaker for a warm-up.

As for lights, it will be necessary to turn off room lights without turning off the current to the projector. This is another item to be checked in advance.

But get everyone properly seated before turning out the lights. Stumbling in the dark can be dangerous!

**TIMING IS IMPORTANT**

Having selected the visual aid that will best serve your purposes, decide on the most effective time for using it. Effectiveness is greatly increased with proper timing.

Consider stopping the projector once or twice for discussion of major points. A work clothes manufacturer averred, "We seldom run a film through without stopping. It's better to halt for a moment and clinch the teaching points covered up to that time. The audience gets much more out of it."

After deciding whether to stop your movie, work up the introductory material—title of the film, background information, type of message, and running time. Be explicit regarding the purpose of it. Suggest that the audience watch for certain things, especially things related to the teaching points. When your salesmen know they're expected to learn certain things, they're more likely to learn them.

# USING AUDIO-VISUAL AIDS EFFECTIVELY

### DEVELOP A COMPETENT PROJECTIONIST

You should arrange for a projectionist. It's too much to conduct the meeting and also operate a projector. Besides, sales executives are seldom skilled as projectionists. Their interests usually point in other directions. If you do not have an assistant who can do a good job with your visual equipment, someone on your staff should be trained. The company that sold the equipment will provide information on its operation and care. Most companies will train the projectionist for you. Many sales meetings are ruined by incompetent projectionists. See that yours becomes an expert. And how about an understudy? Someone else should be trained to the point that he can pinch hit in the absence of the regular projectionist.

"At two consecutive meetings we had trouble with our projector, because no one had been trained to operate it! Both meetings were ruined because of it. Don't let this happen to you," warned a sales manager.

Just one more thing . . . when sales meetings are conducted in rented auditoriums or hotel rooms, the building management may require that a union projectionist be utilized. Check on this in advance. Then you'll have ample time to arrange for a member of the local.

Your company may insist that it has the right to operate its own equipment in spite of building regulations. In such instances, a member of the local need merely be present . . . and paid. Your company personnel can actually run the machine.

### WHAT TO DO AFTER THE SHOWING

Immediately after the showing, summarize the film and review the main ideas. Better still, question the audience. Ask for a summary. Discuss major points. Above all, explain how the information affects the individual. Tell him how he can apply it to his work. Let everyone know what he's expected to do as a result of seeing the film.

"Application is the thing to shoot for," declared a Hartford insurance executive. "If the film doesn't get action for you, it's been a waste of time."

### HOW TO USE THE OPAQUE PROJECTOR

Another visual aid is the opaque projector. This machine is heavy and, therefore, not as portable as other equipment. But it will project any object in true color.

Actual physical specimens can be projected—even an article such as a fountain pen or cigarette lighter. Full sheets of copy, pages from catalogues or magazines, pictures, and other printed matter can be shown. In fact, any object that will reflect light can be shown in semi darkness.

You sometimes have something unusual to show. If it's too small to be seen without enlargement, consider the opaque projector, which is capable of doing many jobs.

### THE VERSATILE OVERHEAD PROJECTOR

The overhead projector is even more versatile. It enables a speaker to face his audience in a fully lighted room while projecting pictures on a screen above and behind him. Also, certain overhead projectors can be adapted to show slides and filmstrips.

Many companies use the overhead projector for training in connection with sales forms and reports. An order form, for example, can be projected for all to see and discuss.

### HOW TO USE THE CHALKBOARD

Time changes everything to some degree. Yet the old fashioned blackboard is still the most widely used visual aid of all. The trend now favors green, tan, or blue colored boards, called chalkboards rather than blackboards. Such boards are excellent for listing points the audience should remember. "Good chalk talks are the backbone of some of our best sales meetings, especially the smaller ones. You give 'em something to see," vowed a Dallas personnel manager. "And to recapture interest, you can strike the board several times with the end of the chalk. It really focuses attention!"

# USING AUDIO-VISUAL AIDS EFFECTIVELY 51

Showmanship and suspense can be utilized through the strip tease technique. Simply write your main points on the board before the meeting starts. Then tape a separate piece of blank paper over each point. The audience is held in suspense until a point is made verbally, at which time you rip off the piece of paper covering the point. Thus you present the point visually as well as verbally.

### Eight Tips for Using Chalkboards Effectively

Pot only major teaching points on the board.
Determine in advance what those points are.
Decide how each point can be summarized.
Write or print rapidly.
When writing keep your side, not your back, toward the audience.
Talk while writing, to avoid a lag. Use colored chalk for variety and showmanship. Do not list the next point until you finish discussing the one preceding it.

### GENERATED CHARTS MAY SUBSTITUTE FOR CHALKBOARDS

A hard-hitting sales executive may feel that a chalkboard smacks of a schoolroom set up. If so, he can use generated charts.

To use generated charts, attach a pad or set of blank charts to an easel. Then, using a crayon or marking pencil, develop the chart while in front of the group. As with a chalkboard, you write as you make your presentation. When one sheet is filled, you flip it over so you can write on the next.

If the information on a sheet must be kept visible longer, tear it off and tape it on the wall. There may be occasions when you'll want to tape several charts on the wall—a combination of good teaching and good showmanship.

"I like to use generated charts," declared a Charlotte, North Carolina executive. "The audience is intrigued because no one can anticipate what I will put on them. Sometimes I even draw cartoons to help illustrate my points."

## HOW TO USE PREPARED CHARTS

Try using prepared charts, sometimes referred to as flow charts. They're mounted in the same manner as generated charts. But the writing on prepared charts is done in advance.

Keep the charts simple. Put only one major idea on each chart. For instance, a single word might be the only thing on a chart making the idea stand out.

For greatest impact, have an artist illustrate the charts and let the drawings tell much of the story, because they will create interest and can easily be remembered. Animated drawings or cartoons are usually best which can be created in less time with less professionalism required.

As you show each page to your audience, be sure to read all the words on it before elaborating. The audience will automatically read all of the copy, regardless of what you do. It's their natural reaction. Having directed their attention to the new sheet, keep your own attention there until you've read it in its entirety. Do otherwise and you lose your audience.

## HOW TO BUILD YOUR POINTS USING A SLAP BOARD

Slap boards are becoming more popular. There are several variations of this tool, but the different types have one thing in common. The speaker literally "slaps" cards, containing his main points, onto a board.

One of the first types in use was the magnetic board, which has a metal front or face, usually covered with a thin fabric. Small flat magnets are mounted on the back of each card. This device is dramatic. The law of gravity seems suddenly to become ineffective! Moreover, it permits the speaker to build up his points one at a time, visually as well as verbally. "We use slap boards in all of our branches," said a chain store official. "The slap of the card keeps the audience alert. Of all types of visuals, we like the slap boards best."

# USING AUDIO-VISUAL AIDS EFFECTIVELY 53

**THE FLOCK BOARD IS AN INNOVATION**

A more recent innovation is the flock board. It's face is covered with a fabric with long loose fibers. Strips of fabric with short stiff fibers are glued to the backs of the cards. When the speaker slaps the cards against the board, there's locking action.

Many people have used flannel or felt for covering the board, hence the terms flannelboard and feltboard. Coarse sandpaper, pasted on the backs of the cards, will adhere to most materials.

Since most executives are not the "do-it-yourself" type, slap boards are seldom improvised. Various kinds and sizes, complete with tripods, can be purchased at commercial audio-visual houses.

But any slap board is more practical when used to support a talk that's given repeatedly. Preparation of cards involves a little effort and expense. Where the same cards are used several times, the investment is proportionately less.

### Six Suggestions for Using Slap Boards

1. Be sure the information printed on the cards is what the audience should remember. No trivia.
2. Consider using some cards containing photographs, dia grams, charts, symbols—anything but plain copy.
3. Practice slapping the cards on the board so there'll be no fumbling during your presentation.
4. Make a last minute check to assure that the cards are ar ranged in sequence of use.
5. Keep each card out of sight until you place it on the board.
6. Face the audience—not the board—as much as possible.

**HOW TO USE A TAPE RECORDER PROFITABLY**

A tape or wire recorder adds zip to a sales meeting. It's useful in producing prerecorded sounds that are not readily available at the location of the meeting.

As an example, let's suppose a V.I.P. is unable to attend. Get a taped message from him and then play it at your meeting.

## 54  USING AUDIO-VISUAL AIDS EFFECTIVELY

Caution: audio without visual can quickly become boring. Use only brief messages. For maximum interest, project a picture of the V.I.P. so that the audience can see him while hearing him.

Recorded music can often improve your staging. A New Jersey sales training manager reports, "I once made a talk on positive thinking. I used a recording of the song "Accentuate The Positive." The music climaxed my speech quite effectively. In fact, I was given a standing ovation!"

Another executive spoke on the future of salesmanship. He used a recording of "I Believe."

Still another used a recording of an automobile wreck, followed by the eerie wail of a siren. It animated his subject, "The Accident That Killed a Sale."

A food supplement concern developed a library of talks that were taped by outstanding sales personalities. The tapes were used time and again at various sales meetings conducted by their salespeople. "This added to the meetings," reported a company official. "I highly recommend a tape library."

A recorder can also be used to present the commentary for a slide or filmstrip series. The preparation of such a series is a big job and is seldom undertaken unless the series will be shown many times. A recorded narration can be played every time the series is projected. This gives a professional flair to the proceedings. It also saves breath!

A company distributing auto parts made different use of a tape recorder. Reports of poor sales meetings emanated from the company's western division. So a recorder was used to monitor the meetings.

A tape of each meeting was sent to the home office. Knowing the "brass" would hear the tapes, the division manager conducted better meetings. And the suggestions he received from the home office made his meetings still better.

**DISPLAYS CREATE THE RIGHT MOOD**

To produce background or setting, use an exhibit. You can display product, literature, merchandising materials, or sales aids.

# USING AUDIO-VISUAL AIDS EFFECTIVELY

Such displays help create the proper atmosphere and mood . . . the right "climate." This preconditions the audience, causing better reception of the material to be presented.

Backdrops related to the theme of the meeting can also serve this purpose. For example, where the Harvest theme is used, displays could include pumpkins, a bale of hay, a shock of grain, and so forth. For the football theme you could display pennants, footballs, helmets, and megaphones.

Don't rush by the exhibit booths the next time you're visiting a trade show. Look at the exhibits. You'll get many ideas for making displays.

When taking in a state fair you can see display after display after display. Many of the principles and techniques used at fairs can be employed in creating your own displays.

### AUDIO-VISUAL AIDS ARE INVALUABLE-USE THEM

As you see, audio-visual aids can do much for sales meetings. They help set the stage, get attention, stimulate interest, and make things clear. They cause teaching points to be grasped more quickly and remembered longer.

Therefore check availability before each meeting, to see which aids can be obtained or improvised. Then determine which ones will best project your message and accomplish your objective.

Work out the details of use—rehearse—in order to have a smooth presentation. The satisfaction that comes from the proper use of audio-visual aids is immeasurable.

**HOW TO USE AUDIO-VISUAL AIDS EFFECTIVELY**

**Work Films Into Meetings Rather Than Meetings Into Films**

**Consider Producing Your Own Films**

**Check All Sources of Audio-Visual Aids**

**Test Projection Equipment Beforehand**

**Use Audio-Visual Aids at the Best Time**

**Develop a Competent Projectionist**

**Introduce Films—Then Summarize**

## 56   *USING AUDIO-VISUAL* **AIDS EFFECTIVELY**

### EMPLOY VARIOUS AUDIO-VISUAL AIDS

| | |
|---|---|
| Moving Pictures | Generated Charts |
| Filmstrips | Prepared Charts |
| **Slides** | Slap Board Flock |
| Opaque Projector | Board Tape |
| Overhead Projector | Recorder Displays |
| Chalkboard | |

# 6. How to Use Speakers to Best Advantage

**MINIMIZE THE AMOUNT OF SPEAKING**

Meetings are often spoiled by too many speeches. There are too many speeches because there are too many speakers. Audiences have been bored to death! You can easily avoid this common error. It's all in the preparation. When *planning* a sales *meeting,* forego *the natural inclination to* review available speaking talent. First, decide on what you want to accomplish. Ask yourself some questions:

What do you want everyone to do as a result of the meeting? Work harder? Sell more merchandise? Improve in certain respects? Develop new techniques?

How can you make them want to do it?

What subject matter will do most toward achieving this?

How can the subject best be presented?

Who knows the most about each subject?

Is he actively and successfully involved in it now?

Can he get it across by doing something other than speaking on it?

Can he demonstrate it? Would role playing be effective? Are suitable audio-visual aids available?

# 58   *HOW TO USE SPEAKERS TO BEST* ADVANTAGE

Should special audio-visual aids be improvised?

What other props would help?

Insist on giving yourself satisfactory answers. You won't have as many speakers but you'll have better meetings. You'll be recognized as a good organizer, a showman, and a top flight sales executive.

## HOW TO SELECT THE RIGHT SPEAKERS

Only about one subject out of three should be covered by a speech. Go heavy on demonstrations. Salesmen want to be shown —not told. Even the speeches should be laced with visuals and enough dramatics to avoid monotony.

But for the speaking that will take place, don't settle for theory. Select speakers who are currently successful in the areas assigned. Use men who are on the firing line, daily faced with their topics. Star salesmen often know more about sales than the presidents of their companies!

The other salesmen will listen to one of their own kind. They'll respect him. They'll never consider him "a company official who's trying to preach at us."

## ROTATE THE SPEAKING ASSIGNMENTS

Be alert to the danger of using the same speakers too often. It's easy to create the feeling that you have a couple of "fair haired boys." Nobody wants the boss's favorites "crammed down his throat."

There's another reason for rotating speaking assignments among several of your stronger men. It's good for their development. A wise executive is continually developing his personnel, and this is an opportunity to do it.

At larger meetings you can't afford to use mediocre speakers. There's too much at stake.

Small meetings require less professionalism. An average salesman might do a creditable job at a small meeting. But look out! The fellow who merely talks a good game won't be respected by

# HOW *TO* USE *SPEAKERS TO BEST* ADVANTAGE        59

the others. Too often he talks about what he wishes he had done, instead of what he's actually doing. The other salesmen realize it, too.

"It hurts more than you think when you use a speaker who's known to be a failure in the field," a company official declared. "Knowing that the one speaker has never set any records, the audience starts wondering if certain other speakers might be poor producers. So you'd better have your best men do the speaking."

#### SHORT TALKS ARE BETTER THAN LONG ONES

Few speakers can interest an audience for more than ten minutes. A talk may glitter at first. As it grows longer, though, it usually becomes dull. Keep talks short. Two brief talks are much better than a long one. To have short talks, divide a subject into two or three parts. Then assign a speaker for each part. For instance, customer service might be divided into two parts—follow-up calls and follow-up correspondence.

Make any logical division of a subject that helps avoid a long boring speech. Secondly, allot only so much time to each speaker.

#### PUCE YOUR STRONGEST SPEAKERS AT CRUCIAL SPOTS

Aim for a good start and a strong close. This helps make any meeting successful.

The same is true of each session within the meeting. The first and last events are important. That being the case, place the best speakers in these crucial spots.

"You'd better have a real stem winder in the final spot—someone who can rock 'em and sock 'em!" This advice came from a Texas insurance executive. It's good advice, too.

#### KEEP THE SUBJECTS IN LOGICAL SEQUENCE

When you spot speakers there's something else to consider. You should arrange a logical sequence of subject matter to permit continuity of thought. It makes for a better meeting.

An example—a speaker on "How To Approach Prospective

Customers" should speak before a demonstration of the product. Another example—a speech on getting new customers should precede a movie on how to keep customers.

In planning your agenda you should have considered the sequence of subject matter (Chapter 2). Stick to your plan. Don't heed someone's request to, "Let me talk first and get it over with."

### PRODUCE A CHANGE OF PACE

Mix them up. Create variety. Sandwich women speakers between men. Place a speaker between a quiz game and a slide series. If at all possible, avoid having two speakers in a row.

### HOW TO GET SPEAKERS TO PREPARE

There's only one way of making certain that a speaker will develop his material. Request an outline of his speech. This prompts him to do some thinking. The value is many-fold . . . The obvious reward is a better talk because of more thorough preparation. More important is the review it affords. You can tell in advance whether there's a good chance of accomplishing the objective of the meeting. An omission of a vital subject can be noted in time to make the desired addition.

You also can detect any overlapping of material. For example, a speaker may consider objections to be nothing more than offered closes. Instead of sticking with objections, then, he would dwell on closing techniques. His material might cover the same ground as the event that follows his talk. Such duplication can be eliminated when outlines are submitted in advance.

Because of these advantages, request outlines of all speakers-even the boss. Specify the deadline well in advance of the meeting. If someone fails to meet the deadline, check with him immediately. This may prevent embarrassment.

### HOW TO HELP YOUR SPEAKERS

There are many things you can do to help speakers. How much *help you should give* will depend upon a number of things. For larger meetings more help should be offered. That's be-

# HOW TO USE SPEAKERS TO BEST ADVANTAGE 61

cause more is expected of a speaker at a large meeting and his task is more difficult.

There's also more reason to help if the speaker has an extremely important subject. The length of his talk is a factor, too. The longer the talk, the more chance that he will bog down.

Another consideration is the amount of help he's willing to accept. A few speakers know it all—or think they do. They'll accept little help. Others will listen to your suggestions but forget them the moment the meeting begins. Trying to help such fellows is a waste of time. Expend your energy on those who will accept direction.

### WHAT EVERY SPEAKER SHOULD KNOW ABOUT FEAR

There's little reason for a speaker to be afraid. More people have died in the audience than at the speaker's platform! Besides, the speaker knows more about his speech than anyone else. So why should he be afraid?

Most speakers do experience fear, however. And a little apprehension is good. It causes the individual to be keyed up, and as a result, he actually does a better job. Nervousness helps him rise to the occasion. Without stimulation his delivery would be flat and the speech, a miserable flop.

Some speakers develop real jitters—stage fright! They're tense, yet they shiver and shake. Their voices are shrill and trembling. Their gestures are stilted. Some are so tight they make no gestures. Still worse, they can't think as well. They're dazed—even a little confused.

When a speaker is this conscious of himself, he cannot make his best talk. His natural reaction is to end the agony as soon as possible. This causes him to speed along in an ineffective manner. He doesn't communicate with his audience. He merely exposes his message.

### THE CAUSE OF FEAR

The cause of such fear is easily explained. It stems from a series of experiences that have undermined his self-confidence.

# 62 HOW TO USE *SPEAKERS TO BEST* ADVANTAGE

The first of these unfortunate events may have occurred when the individual was only one or two years old. Often there's some small thing the parents do, or fail to do, which creates insecurity. Next, an older brother or sister shows superiority in front of others. This makes him feel inadequate. A cutting remark from a teacher shakes him up a little more. Confusion regarding sex makes him even less sure of himself.

A bad complexion, hand-me-down clothes, a skeleton in the family closet—many things destroy confidence. Thus, stage fright is very deep rooted.

The speaker can't relive his life. Even if he could, he'd have many of the same shattering experiences. Several things can be done, however, to reduce his fear at the speakers' stand.

### 15 Ways to Combat Fear

1. *Request him to make the talk.* Don't direct him to do so. When he tackles it voluntarily, he puts more "heart" into it. His confidence is greater. You're no longer the only one who believes he's capable. He also thinks he can do it. A San Diego bank cashier said, "The first time I was selected to speak at a meeting, I was told I had to speak. Having been drafted regardless of how I felt about it, I was terrified! A fellow should be asked to speak. He'll feel better about it."

2. *Ask him well in advance.* This gives him time to get used to the idea. It also enables him to research his subject, to organize his material, and to practice delivery. These things make for self-confidence and self-assurance. "Before making my first speech, I had six weeks' notice. This helped, because I not only had time to get used to the idea, but I had time to get help from several friends." These words come from a farm implement dealer who is now an accomplished speaker.

3. *Recommend* appropriate *visuals and other aids.* If the speaker is a salesman, he's busy keeping "the body in front of the prospect." He has little time for planning ways of spicing his speech. Suggest visual and other aids. Help him integrate some

# HOW TO USE SPEAKERS *TO* BEST ADVANTAGE 63

good props. Then watch his confidence grow. A magazine crew manager said, "I always feel better if I have one or two good things to show during my talk. I know the audience will at least like that part of my talk."

4. Show confidence *in his* material. Having received an outline of his talk, acknowledge it with enthusiasm. Assure him he will cover the points of greatest need and interest. Tell him his talk will be quite favorably received. "After the boss said he liked my material, I figured everyone would," confessed a dealer of auto mobile parts. "This made me much more willing to take the stand at our last sales meeting."

5. Offer *to get his notes typed.* Typewritten words can be read more easily. Use large type. If jumbo type is not available, the typist can put everything in "caps." Triple space for still easier reading. "Nothing is worse than notes that are difficult to read. Notes written in pencil are usually quite difficult to read under the light on the speakers' stand. Use typewritten notes." These are the words of an experienced lecturer. Do not hyphenate a word, completing it on the next line. This makes the use of notes more obvious. The same can be said of a sentence that starts at the bottom of one page and ends at the top of the next.

6. Urge him *to practice.* The better he knows his material, the more confidence he will have in his ability to deliver it. If he's only gone over it a couple of times, he should be afraid. At least five practice efforts are recommended. They'll work like magic in reducing fear. "Maybe I'm an old maid," vowed a corporation president in Idaho. "But I keep practicing until I can't miss. I believe it's worth the effort or I wouldn't do it."

7. Eliminate his stumbling *blocks.* A speaker often stumbles at the same place each time. This is because certain words and phrases are difficult for him to pronounce. Help your speaker reword trouble spots. Then he'll have material he can master, giving him greater confidence. Unless this is done, he will stumble again at the same place when "the chips are down." And nothing upsets a speaker more than a mistake that is obvious to both him and his audience. He loses composure, and having become

rattled, he may very well stumble again. Then he's in trouble! For instance, if he has difficulty saying, "four or five frequencies," have him change it to, "at least four frequencies."

8. *Call for a dress* rehearsal. Ask the speaker to "dry run" all costuming, props, and other aids. Many little things can go wrong. Each visual or prop is a potential trouble maker. By working out details of their use, the speaker gains confidence. "Our sales manager insists on a dress rehearsal," said a Washington, D.C. salesman. "At first it seemed silly, but it has helped all of us who have participated in the meetings. The rehearsals reduce fear."

9. *Check the need for "refinders."* Occasionally the speaker will leave his notes for a few minutes. He may walk to the chalk board, or step aside for a demonstration. Any such break in the routine throws him off pace. When he returns to the lectern, he finds it difficult to resume the use of notes and takes several seconds to find the proper place. This delay is embarrassing and causes him to lose poise. To avoid this, advise him to use "refinders." This is, have him mark his notes so he can readily find his place again. A star in the margin of his notes will do the job. Then he won't lose time and confidence after each departure.

10. Have *him get the feel of the rostrum.* Anyone not familiar with the speakers' stand should visit it before the meeting. He can determine how to handle his notes, can see if they'll stay in place. He gets an idea of how the room looks from the platform. He can visualize the audience. Then, when he jumps up to make his talk, he's acquainted with the surroundings and much more sure of himself. As a consequence, he will have less fear. "This has done more to help me than anything else," a Wichita man declared. "I realize now I had been afraid of the speakers' stand. I didn't want to visit the stand . . . not even *before* the meeting. But now I have no fear at all."

11. *Don't remind him that big shots will be* there. The speaker may have complexes regarding certain "big-wigs." In short, he's afraid of the "brass." It probably dates back to a "chewing" that he's not forgotten, but why remind him of it? Silence can be golden.

A public speaking teacher said, "A few people like to show off

## HOW TO USE *SPEAKERS TO BEST* ADVANTAGE 65

before the boss. But most speakers are apprehensive if the boss is present. Even I feel less sure of myself if the president of the college is in the audience when I'm making a speech. So don't play up the presence of company officials. It makes your speaker less sure of himself."

12. *Give* a pep-talk prior *to the meeting.* Rendezvous with all speakers shortly before kick-off time, to answer any last minute questions. Inspire them by telling briefly of over-all plans. Let them know there'll be a sequence of subject matter. Tell them a variety of events will be staged. Assure them there's no duplication of material. Then close on an encouraging note. "Let's top all previous meetings. We can do it—let's go get 'em!"

"I'm no Knute Rockne," said a Monroe, North Carolina sales leader. "But my pep talks inspire confidence, if nothing else. Give 'em a try. You'll be glad you did."

13. Make *him take a few deep breaths.* Deep breathing relaxes the respiration system and reduces tension in the right places. While a "pro" is being introduced, watch him closely. You'll see him breathe deeply three or four times before taking the stand. This reduces symptoms of fear, which, in turn, reduces fear itself. A speaker from Kansas City does push-ups before taking the stand! "They relax me," he said. "I get behind a screen and do a few push-ups. As someone once quipped, 'Don't knock it if you haven't tried it!'"

14. *Let him do a solo.* He can't feel comfortable when you seat people behind him. It's bad enough to seat people on either side. A St. Paul merchant said, "When people are sitting behind me, I become conscious of them. I try to look at them from time to time. When I do, I lose contact with the rest of the audience. It's no good!" If at all possible, put the total audience in one place. Any speaker will be less apprehensive. He'll be more capable, too.

15. *Bring him on with a* bang/ See that he's introduced in an enthusiastic way. Let everyone know he's a great guy. Explain why he's qualified to handle the subject. This gives him that last-second certainty. Also, the emcee should wait for him to reach the stand. A handshake and verbal pat on the back are encouraging. "I'll never forget the moment I got up to speak," reported

the owner of a greeting card company. "The emcee gave me that last moment boost that I needed. He acted as if the sales meeting would finally be a success now that I was about to speak. It helped!"

### HOW TO KEEP THE ATTENTION OF A LARGE AUDIENCE

A conversational tone is used in talking with another fellow. It won't keep his attention very long, however. His mind wanders sooner or later. Finally he interrupts with a thought of his own, proving that normal tone and volume are inadequate.

Since a normal speaking voice isn't enough to keep the interest of one person, it certainly won't keep the interest of a group.

Yet the novice speaker uses a conversational tone before an audience. He talks as if only one or two people were listening. Before long there are only one or two people listening. The others have lost interest!

To keep the attention of a group, the speaker must project himself. He must extend his personality. His voice and his words must be strongly planted in the far corners of the room. He must leave his "shell" to capture the imagination of the people sitting in the last row.

This is done through dramatics, particularly voice projection.

A professional trainer said, "Anyone who wants to speak convincingly before large audiences must learn voice projection. You absolutely cannot be forceful without it."

### HOW A SPEAKER CAN PROJECT HIS VOICE

Anyone can project his voice by using greater volume. He concentrates on the people in the rear of the room. If *they* can get the message, everyone can.

He depends less on the public address system, backing away from the mike to avoid deafening the audience. His words are spoken more slowly than usual. He forces out phrases and sentences as if they're the product of profound thought. He's both deliberate and distinct.

The tone of his voice is higher than usual. Yet it's far from shrill.

# HOW TO USE SPEAKERS TO BEST ADVANTAGE 67

Speaking from the chest instead of his throat, he produces a robust quality.

His talk becomes a declaration. When he really gets hot, it sounds like an ultimatum!

#### WHEN TO USE VOICE PROJECTION

Voice projection should always be used with groups exceeding 50 people. It helps overrule distractions. The speaker becomes more dynamic, more penetrating. Each member of the audience feels that the message is more personal—is intended for him. It's like magic!

A good example of voice projection can be found at the national political conventions. The politicians really extend their voices! Instead of starting with, "Mr. Chairman," they say, "M-I-S-T-E-R C-H-A-I-R-M-A-NM"

When arranging a large sales meeting, show your speakers how to project their voices. Have them try out under your supervision. All practice efforts should be without benefit of a p.a. system, because this will condition the speakers to use ample volume.

Advise them to "let go!" The speaking platform is no place for self-restraint.

### HOW TO USE SPEAKERS TO BEST ADVANTAGE

Minimize the Amount of Speaking

Select the Right Speakers

Rotate Speaking Assignments

Schedule Short Talks Instead of Long Ones

Place Your Strongest Speakers at Crucial Spots

Keep the Subjects in Logical Sequence

Produce a Change of Pace Get

Your Speakers to Prepare Help

Those Who Will Accept It

Assist in Reducing Fear

Encourage Voice Projection

# 7.  How to Organize a Speech

Unless a speaker has had special training, his talk may be poorly planned. The natural tendency is to jot down various facts on the subject, making little effort to organize these facts. Then a few funny stories are added, usually at the beginning. The humor probably could be tied into the rest of the material, but often it is not.

When delivering his talk, the speaker tries for a laugh or two. Then he plunges into a maze of unorganized information. The result of it all is a poor speech.

Enough of the wrong way—here's the right method. Here's the way speakers at your sales meetings can organize their speeches ...

**HOW TO COLLECT MATERIAL FOR A TALK**

Subjects should be assigned well in advance. This enables your speaker to collect his material. He first should consider researching it. Does he have complete information or can he learn a great deal more about it? Should he "read up" on it? Should he ask others about it? Can he better acquaint himself with it through actual practice?

From time to time, pertinent facts will come to mind. Your speaker should not trust his memory. He should write down these thoughts as they occur. Over a period of several days, many ideas can be collected. It's difficult, on the other hand, to dig all the ideas out of the subconscious at one time.

If he must do heavy research, you've probably picked the wrong man. Most speakers should investigate their subjects, however. Mere reflection will produce ideas but is not always adequate.

# HOW TO ORGANIZE A SPEECH

## HOW TO DECIDE UPON THE POINT OF A TALK

After collecting material on his subject, the speaker should decide what point he wants to make.

The point is the one main idea. It's the most important part of the talk and other parts merely serve in clinching the point.

To determine his point, the speaker considers the interests of his audience. Who will attend? What are their interests in the subject? Exactly what are their needs in that connection? How can a speech help them?

Specifically, what should they do as a result of the speech? What's the point to be made—the thing they should do after it's all over. For example, if the speaker wants more enthusiasm shown then his point might be, "Let's have enthusiasm!"

Inexperienced speakers often try to make too many points. Unless the talk is lengthy, one point is all that can be put across. The speaker is going after "big game." Therefore, he should use a powerful rifle instead of a scatter gun. It's better to drive home one good idea than to mention several points without clinching any of them.

## HOW TO DETERMINE WHETHER THE POINT IS APPROPRIATE

Having decided on the point to be made, the speaker then determines whether he can justify it.

He asks himself why the point is correct. Why should the audience accept it? What will it do for the audience?

Then he makes a list of these things. By reviewing the list, the speaker can decide whether he's sold on his point. If he's not fully sold, he should select a different point. He could never hope to sell his audience if he cannot even sell himself!

Reasons for the point might include such things as:

> "It will save you time."
>
> "It will make your job easier."
>
> "It will enable you to get more customers."
>
> "It will help you make bigger sales."
>
> "It will put dollars in your pockets."

## HOW TO DEVELOP THE MEAT OF A TALK

Once he has selected a point he can justify, the speaker develops examples. These examples are the meat of the talk. They show how the point works, where it works, when it works, for whom it has already worked. At least half of the entire talk is devoted to examples. The audience is told exactly how to employ the one major idea.

Typical examples are:

"This idea was first used about a year ago, and has since worked quite well."

"Then Bob Stevens used it. He found that it worked with every customer."

"It's good to use where the sale. . . ."

"And it's especially effective when utilized as. . . ."

"Further, the time for using it is now, when you. . . ."

## HOW TO PREPARE THE CLOSE OF A TALK

The speaker has decided on a point, has convinced himself that the point is a good one, and has developed examples to show how it works. Now he's ready to prepare the close.

When closing, the speaker restates his main idea. He returns to his point briefly but convincingly and makes a plea for action. This last step is begun with such words as, "So I say"; "So be sure to . . ."

A speaker at a Sales Executives Club Meeting concluded his talk on positive thinking with: "Therefore, let's think positively. Negative thoughts are poisonous. Whereas, positive thoughts produce sales. Think positively about your job, think positively about your merchandise, and think positively about your salesmen. Then you have a right to think positively about your future."

This type of close clears up any misunderstanding about the main point. Also, it leaves the point uppermost in the mind of everyone. The audience knows what is expected as a consequence of the talk. In short, it "wraps everything up in a neat package."

# HOW TO ORGANIZE A SPEECH

## HOW TO WORK OUT THE BEGINNING OF A TALK

The speech is now complete except for the beginning. This means that the opening statements are prepared last.

There's good reason for putting first things last. The main point deserves prior consideration because it is more important. The opening remarks merely serve in getting people receptive to the point of the talk.

Many speakers begin their talks with jokes. It's true that a few funny stories will soften the audience. Jokes help settle everyone down, including the speaker. Usually, though, some humor should be saved for the body of the talk. To put all the humor in the first minute or so, is amateurish. The audience expects a light and enjoyable presentation, only to be disappointed.

Questions are sometimes used to begin a speech. They "open" the mind.

Other speakers use something loud, dramatic, or unusual. Any type of opener can be used, provided two requirements are met ... The beginning of the talk must (1) command attention, and (2) lead smoothly into the point.

Rarely will an opener automatically lead to the point. The speaker must make it connect. He will build a bridge from the interest-getter to his main idea. He can easily do this with such words as, "Perhaps you're wondering what this means and how it applies to you. Well, here's the whole idea—the one big point I'd like to make. It means that . . ."

All five steps have now been covered. Since these five steps are important, here they are again in brief:

### A BIRD'S-EYE VIEW OF THE FIVE-STEP PLAN

Decide Upon the Point

Determine Whether It's Appropriate

Develop Examples of What, How, When, Where It Works

Restate the Point With a Plea for Action

Work up an Interest Getter

Now the speaker is ready to arrange his material in the order in which he will deliver it. This can be done simply by moving the interest-getter from the bottom of the list to the top.

**WHY THE FIVE-STEP PLAN IS SO EFFECTIVE**

The foregoing five-step plan works wonders! It places enough emphasis on the one main idea so that the audience remembers it. Many will take action, which is still more significant.

There's another reason why this five-step plan is so effective. It's based on consideration of the audience and automatically answers questions that may arise in the minds of the persons listening.

**HOW AUDIENCE REACTION IS TAKEN INTO ACCOUNT**

For example, when a speaker is introduced, some people in the audience are indifferent. They ask themselves, "Why should I listen to him? Hope he doesn't talk too long. Isn't there something else I should be doing?" But the speaker's interest-getter crashes through the barrier of indifference—it makes the audience want to listen.

When their attention has been captured, they start wondering, "So what? This doesn't affect me, does it?" The point answers such questions. It pins things down and gives listeners the specific idea for which they are now ready.

After the point has been made, people want reasons or justification for it. They're thinking, "Why? Why should we do that, or why is that true—just because he says it?" So it is logical to give reasons for the point. The reasons help sustain interest and sell the major idea.

By this time the audience is thinking, "Sounds okay so far, but how would it work in actual practice? Is it just theory, or is there proof of it?" The speaker holds the audience by giving examples which answer their questions. He supplies the who, where, when and how—the information the audience wants.

At this point the audience knows what to do and how to do it-All that's needed is the inspiration to take action. By returning

# HOW TO ORGANIZE A SPEECH

to the point and closing on a high note, the speaker climaxes the speech in a manner that inspires action. Thus, the audience is left with a feeling of completeness and satisfaction. Listeners are given the information they want at the right time—from the beginning of the speech to the close.

### SIMPLICITY MAKES IT EASY TO USE

Many items for the home are delivered in factory packaging and must be assembled by the purchaser. The instructions for assembling often state "So simple that even a child can do it." But most of us aren't children. Maybe that's why we sometimes have trouble! Or perhaps the assembling is sometimes not simple at all, any plan should be so simple that people can use it. That's another feature of this five-step plan for organizing a speech. It's quite simple. People speaking at one of your sales meetings can learn how to use it in no time at all.

Here's a summary of a speech. It shows the logic and simplicity of this plan:

### CALL BACKS

**Interest-getter:** "This afternoon a man dropped dead in my office! I was startled and shocked!

"Perhaps you knew him. He was a merchant, and one of you tried to sell him our line of goods. He was overstocked at the moment, so he bought nothing. He said he'd buy a couple of weeks later. And he would have bought, had the salesman returned, because he liked our products. He liked them so well he refused to buy any other line.

"But our salesman never returned, so the merchant ran completely out of merchandise. With nothing to sell, he soon lost his store. Then he had no income at all. Finally the poor fellow starved to death.

"Just before dying, he visited me to ask why the salesman never returned. That's how he happened to die in my office.

***Point:*** "A ridiculous story? Of course it is. But sometimes we do fail to call back. And that's the main

# 74 HOW *TO* ORGANIZE A SPEECH

point I'm trying to get across. *Let's make call backs—lots of call backs! Call back* early and often/"

***Reasons for Point:*** "Why? Because a well-timed, follow-up is good salesmanship. Call backs pay off. They always have and they always will. They bring you more customers, bigger sales, and more commissions.

**Examples:** "For example, when you call back on the merchant who has never bought your line, you make him feel important. And sometimes you can get an order from him.

"Where a merchant is already using your line, call backs produce still more sales. The customer is impressed by your sincere desire to serve and, therefore, gives you more of his business.

"We've found that call backs can most easily be made when . . ."

"There'll be times when your call backs should instead be made . . .

"And it's sometimes a good idea to make call backs even though the customer . . ."

**Restate *with Plea For Action:*** "So let's make call backs—frequent call backs. That's what the highest paid salesmen are doing, and it's what all of us should do. Make call backs!"

Here are a couple of brief speeches illustrating the five-step plan:

## GOALS

**Interest-getter:** "Fifty or sixty men were sitting in the room that day. Yet, not a word was being spoken.

"Somewhere in the background I could hear a clock ticking-away the minutes. But except for the ticking of the clock, there was a deafening hush.

"The situation could be likened to that of a company of soldiers, in their last few moments of silence before jumping-off into combat against the enemy. It was surprising to me, because the sales meetings I had attended were full of talk, pep, and enthusiasm.

"Yet, I can almost see them now, each with a pencil and a piece of paper in his hand. They were

# HOW TO ORGANIZE A SPEECH 75

apparently poring over some problems but saying nothing.

"Then, it struck me! I knew what was going on! Because one man jumped from his seat and shouted, 'I'm going to have a 30 percent increase this year!' Another man declared, I'm going to open 30 new accounts by the first of June!'

"That's what those men were doing. They were establishing their objectives. They were setting their goals.

**Point:** "All good salesmen set goals for themselves. *Set your goal today—now/* Set your goal and stick to it! Determine what you expect to accomplish this year. Establish an objective. Then work to reach that objective.

**Reasons for Point:** "How can anyone expect to hit the bull's eye unless he has a target at which to shoot?

"How can you accomplish anything unless you know exactly what it is you plan to accomplish?

"Since salesmanship first became a science, it has been known that goals are essential for success. That's why you should set your goals. They help you succeed.

"Think back to the last time you telephoned Western Union to send a telegram. It's a good bet that, before making the call, you jotted down the exact words to be included in the message. And when you did, you set a goal, because it became your intent to transmit those words and no others.

"Now think back to the last time you went grocery shopping. Did the wife give you a list? When you accepted it from her, you set a goal. It became your objective to go to the store, obtain those items, and return home with them.

"The next man who leaves this room, and gets into an automobile will have a goal. He'll not wander aimlessly around town. He will know exactly where he's going.

"Now then, if we have goals for such simple things as sending telegrams, grocery shopping, and

| | |
|---|---|
| | routine automobile trips, does it not follow that we should set goals for ourselves in this—the cause to which we have dedicated ourselves—our careers with Life Line Insurance Company? |
| **Examples:** | "Of course it does! And that's what the successful salesmen are doing. They're setting goals, and determining what must be done in order to reach those goals.<br><br>"For instance, Cliff Gregory set, as his goal, the Million-Dollar-Round-Table. To reach that goal he calculated that he must write a certain amount of business each month. Thus far he's right on schedule. And he says this goal is the major reason for his success.<br><br>"Then there's Jim Baker. He figured that his goal should be based on earnings. Although he was interested in renewals and future income, he set a goal in connection with earnings for the current year. Yesterday he dropped by the office and reported his progress. He said that this year's earnings will be the highest he has ever enjoyed. Why? Because he had the gumption to set a goal and work to reach it.<br><br>"Another case in point, is Walter Arnold. He set a goal last year but failed to reach it. The difficulty was that he neglected to break down the goal into bite-size chunks. He failed to decide what must be done each month, each week, each day, in order to reach his goal.<br><br>"But this year he broke the goal down into a step-by-step plan. Is it working for him? You bet it is! He's having a tremendous year.<br><br>"So let's be guided accordingly. Setting a goal is not enough. We must break it down into steps that can be taken one at a time. |
| **Restate with Plea For Action:** | "Take a tip from the top producers. Set a goal. Set a goal now! Then break it down into a step-by-step plan.<br>"You'll be better organized. You'll write more business. You'll make more money. "This one act on your part can mean the dif- |

# HOW TO ORGANIZE A SPEECH

ference between success and mediocrity. Set a goal. Now!"

## SEE THE PEOPLE

**Interest-getter:** "At daybreak one morning, two lumberjacks started chopping down trees.

"They chopped and chopped, until the middle of the morning when one of them paused for a moment to sharpen his axe, the other not taking time to do so.

"They continued chopping and chopping, until mid-afternoon when that same lumberjack stopped to sharpen his axe—the other, again, not taking time to do so.

"They continued chopping and chopping, until the sun had fallen in the sky and the forest was cloaked in darkness. At the end of the day, which of the two lumberjacks had felled the more trees?

"Yes, the one who stopped momentarily to sharpen his axe. And that, ladies and gentlemen, is what we are doing today at this sales meeting. We're pausing momentarily to sharpen our axes. We're sharpening our axes for this new year—the biggest year in the history of Ajax Tool!

*Point:* "And this can be your big year with Ajax if you'll only SEE THE PEOPLE. See them early. See them late. See anybody and everybody.

"See them up the street, down the street, across the street. See your in-laws, the outlaws, the dog catcher—see everybody who might buy your merchandise.

**Reasons for Point:** "Make lots of calls, because it's the only way to sell lots of merchandise. Prospecting pays dividends.

"There's a direct relationship between the number of calls and the number of sales.

**Examples:** "For instance, our sales records show that it takes four calls to average one sale. So if you want more sales per week, make more calls per week. If you want one more sale, make four more calls. If you want two more sales, make eight more calls. It's that simple! Purely a matter of mathematics.

"A fellow working from our Bangor office was ready to quit last year. He said he wasn't making enough money. And he was right. He wasn't making enough money.

"We helped him plan his calls so that travel time would be minimized. Also, we urged him to make calls up to 4:50 p.m. instead of 'knocking off' at 4:00 or 4:30. These two factors enabled him to make 12 more calls per month. Those calls resulted in three extra sales per month. Now he's making $1,100 per month instead of $800 per month. He's happy.

"I'll let you in on a secret. We've been working on the profile of a successful salesman. That is, we've been trying to determine what the most successful salesmen look like, how they eat, act, and what they do. We thought this study might help us in selecting salesmen in the future.

"We checked the record at all seventeen branches. In every instance, the same thing stood out: the most successful salesman was the man who made the most calls. There was not a single exception to the rule.

"Here's another illustration. At a civic auditorium sales-rally the other night, our competitor presented an award to one of his salesmen. After receiving the award, the salesman was asked to tell how he'd won it. His speech was brief and pithy: 'Get the body in front of the prospect. That's what I did.' "

**Restate** *with* **Plea** "The best product in the world must be sold.
**For Action:** People won't come to you and take it away from you. You must go to them.

"It's been said that the world will beat a path to your door if you'll build a better mousetrap. But that's not true! Here's a picture of the man who did it. (Show picture of bearded tramp in front of lean-to in a hobo jungle.)

"Does he look prosperous? Is the world beating a path to his door? Of course not! He must see the people.

"And we must see the people. We don't have

# HOW TO ORGANIZE A SPEECH 79

a better mousetrap. We have something even greater! But it won't sell itself. Let's see the people!

## IT'S ALSO THE NATURAL THING TO DO

"For the proof of its logic and simplicity, let's suppose your wife is leaving home to do the family shopping. It would be natural for you to yell, 'Hey, Mary! Get some coffee. We're nearly out. There's not enough for breakfast tomorrow. Besides, we'll want some with dinner tonight. So be sure to get coffee.' "

| | |
|---|---|
| Interest-getter: | "Hey, Mary" |
| *Point:* | "Get some coffee." |
| Reasons for Point: | "We're nearly out." |
| Examples: | "There's not enough for breakfast tomorrow. Besides, we'll want some with dinner tonight." |
| Restate *with Plea* For Action: | "So be sure to get coffee." |

## HOW TO PUT ACROSS MORE THAN ONE POINT

Long talks should usually be avoided. Few speakers can keep the attention of an audience more than 10 or 15 minutes. It's a cinch the speaker cannot inspire action when he can't even keep attention.

It takes 10 or 15 minutes to clinch a point—that is, to drive it home properly. Therefore, a speaker should seldom try to make more than one point. When more than one point is to be made, however, the five-step plan can still be used.

The five steps are observed in putting across each point. For example, the speaker goes through the five steps in making his first point. Then he repeats the five-step procedure for each additional point.

## HOW TO GET YOUR SPEAKERS TO USE THE PLAN

Some of your speakers will need help in organizing their speeches. Explain this plan to them. Urge them to use it. Sell tie benefits.

Indecision and change of decision in speech planning will be cut to a minimum. They'll save precious time. Having organized a couple of speeches in this way, they'll never go back to the slipshod method.

Poor talks have done more to ruin sales meetings than any other one thing. While you can minimize the amount of speaking and number of speeches, some talking is always necessary. In every possible instance, get the speakers to use the five-step plan in organizing their material. Their talks will be more interesting and effective.

Result: Your sales meeting will undoubtedly be improved.

**HOW TO ORGANIZE A SPEECH**

**Collect Material for the Talk**

**Decide Upon the Point**

**Determine Whether the Point Is Appropriate**

**Develop Examples—The Meat of the Talk**

**Restate the Point, Making a Plea for Action**

**Work Up an Interest-getter**

# 8  How to Put Humor Into a Speech

A talk at a sales meeting should ordinarily contain some humor. Granted—the purpose of the talk is not to entertain. But a few laughs make the rest of the talk more palatable.

Even the highly-paid professional speakers may depend upon humor to sell the remainder of a speech. In fact, they use humor to a greater degree than speakers who are less skilled. Since the silver-tongued "pros" must use it, the less articulate should consider doing likewise.

"We have an outside speaker at most of our large meetings," reported a Memphis sales executive. "It's usually a 'big man/ someone who can attract a sizeable crowd. And, of course, such a person is a skilled public speaker, but with all his skill, he invariably depends upon humor. Without some good jokes, his effectiveness would be questionable."

Suggest to your speakers that they use a little humor. It keeps your sales meetings from being so "dry." Not everyone can tell a joke well. But everyone can learn to do so. Joke telling can be compared with any other skill. For instance, it can be compared with the ability to use a typewriter. Not everyone knows how to type, but everyone who wants to do so, can learn.

## HOW TO BECOME A GOOD STORY TELLER

To become skilled at telling a funny story, one should know the basis for humor. He should know why people are expected to laugh at a joke. Armed with this knowledge, he can more effectively appeal to the reason for laughing.

The basis of nearly every joke will fall in one or more of four categories:

1. Man's inhumanity to man.
2. A natural target.
3. The unexpected.
4. Sex.

Let's discuss each of these. First, what is meant by man's inhumanity to man?

### Man's Inhumanity to Man

Most of us like to laugh at the other fellow. It makes us feel superior and feeds our egos. Thus, most people laugh at the fellow who's bashed in the face with a gooey pie or who's the butt of a story. It's a little cruel to laugh at the plight of the other fellow, but usually we do.

For example, there's the story about a man who owed some money to his next-door neighbor. He couldn't pay the debt so, naturally, he was worried. His wife kept telling him not to worry, but the man worried anyway.

Finally the wife said, "You don't have to worry. I'll show you. . ."

She went to a window and yelled to the neighbor, "Hey, Fred! Do you remember that $100 my husband borrowed from you? Well, he can't pay you. He's dead broke!"

She slammed down the window and turned to her husband. "See there? You don't have to worry. Let him worry!"

An audience will roar at this joke. The laughter is basically directed at the neighbor. There's no reason why the audience should dislike the neighbor. He had done nothing wrong. Yet the audience will howl at his dilemma. Why? Because of man's inhumanity to man.

Knowing why the audience laughs, you can tell a story more

effectively. You can make the butt of the yarn look as ridiculous and stupid as possible. This increases the mirth!

### A Natural Target

A tyrant is a natural target. For example, many stories belittling dictators have been told through the years. People laugh because of their contempt for the villain. They get pleasure in seeing him ridiculed.

Another example is a story on a mother-in-law. The latter is proverbially a meddlesome individual. Therefore, people laugh at seeing her taken to task: "I'm here before you with mixed emotions. Sorry about one thing and glad about another. I'm like the fellow who saw his beautiful new car roll off a cliff, with his mother-in-law inside!"

A competitor or his product is a natural target. A wise salesman won't berate his competitor when talking to a prospect. But there's nothing wrong with getting in a "dig" or two at a sales meeting.

For instance, "A salesman for one of those cheap imitative products dropped by the other day. He said, 'The price you're getting for your merchandise is atrocious!'

"I told him, 'I can see why you think as you do. For merchandise like yours, the price we're getting really would be atrocious!'"

Adding more coals to the fire: "We know what our product is worth and it is priced accordingly. We presume that the imitators know what their merchandise is worth, and we give them credit for pricing *it* accordingly!"

Having fully realized that you're aiming at a natural target, you can fire your guns more effectively. Your choice of words should show contempt. Your tone of voice should ridicule. The audience will be delighted!

Be sure your natural target is not present at the meeting. For instance, at a department store sales meeting, the merchandise manager told a joke on an old maid (another natural target). Many people laughed. But the old maids didn't!

### The Unexpected

People can be made to laugh when surprised. Apparently it's fun to be fooled, because the unexpected has been the basis for many jokes. For instance . . .

"A man was on top of a tall building, ready to jump off. A policeman saw him and said, 'Hey, wait a minute! You don't want to do that. Let's talk this thing over.'

"So they talked it over for three or four minutes. Then they *both* jumped off!"

### OR

"A sales trainer had finished a lecture and was attempting to start group discussion. He asked for questions or comments, but none were forthcoming. Again he asked, 'Questions or comments, if you will please.' But a deadly silence ensued.

"When everyone became a bit embarrassed, the trainer quipped, 'All right. Thank you very much for all those fine questions and comments. Now we'll go on to the next subject.' "

The audience laughed. The tension was broken. A lively discussion followed, simply because the trainer had said the unexpected.

Another illustration: "Everyone on this side of the room who likes pie, please raise your hand . . . if you like ice cream, raise your hands." The speaker points to one side of the room, then the other. "I now pronounce you pie a la mode!"

They'll laugh gustily, since it's the unexpected.

When selling a laugh on this basis, make the turn of events as completely unexpected as possible. Phrase your remarks in such a way that the audience is taken fully by surprise. You then have maximum effectiveness.

### Sex

Since the day of Adam and Eve, sex has served as the foundation for funny stories. The sex urge is both fundamental and intriguing. Since you've doubtless heard many jokes on the subject, elaborating hardly seems necessary.

# HOW TO PUT HUMOR INTO A SPEECH

Here's one that regales an audience: "Years ago I was working in a little country store when a lady came in, who wanted to buy a dress. Having selected one, she asked if she might try it on.

"As I said, it was a little country store. We didn't have a dressing room. We had simply a curtain in the rear of the building.

"The lady stepped behind the curtain, and I handed her the dress. At that moment the boss walked up and said, 'Bill, if I catch you trying to peek while this lady tries on that dress, I'm going to fire you!'

"Now, after I lost that job . . . (!)"

The foregoing leaves something to the imagination. This is much preferred to an uncouth story or one containing profanity. Vulgarity cheapens any story. In effect, it weakens the position of the speaker; it depreciates him in the mind of the audience.

A professional speaker has often told of a food salesman, a liquor salesman, and a mattress salesman. The food salesman said, "I hate to see a woman dine alone." The liquor salesman said, "If there's anything I hate, it's to see a woman drink alone."

And the mattress salesman said not a word!

## HOW TO HAVE A DOUBLE BARREL APPEAL

Often a story can be based upon two of the four reasons for laughing. This increases its effectiveness.

To illustrate: "At one of our sales meetings, a fellow flinched every time an automobile horn was sounded on the street. He jumped so much that he disturbed the other salesmen. So we stopped the meeting and asked him for an explanation.

"He said, 'A few days ago, my wife ran away with our chauffeur. Every time I hear an automobile horn, I'm afraid it's that chauffeur bringing her back!'"

There's a double sock there. First, the unexpected is spoken. Then there's man's inhumanity to man. The audience howls because the fellow might get his wife back when he obviously wishes she would "drop dead."

Analyze the basis for humor in each story before telling it. If it has two platforms for laugh-getting, tell it in such a way that you fully capitalize on both foundations.

### HOW TO HANDLE THE PUNCH LINE

The final sentence or phrase of a joke is referred to as the "punch line." It's the part that prompts the audience to laugh.

Be very sure that your punch line is worded correctly. The audience must understand its relationship to your build-up, otherwise there's no punch.

For instance, at a sales meeting a speaker told of:

"A farmer was passing an insane asylum with a wagon load of fertilizer. An inmate called out, 'Hey! Where are you going with that fertilizer?'

"The farmer replied, 'To put it on my strawberries.'

"'That's funny,' said the inmate. 'I put sugar and cream on mine.'"

The speaker got a laugh, but it could have been better. His punch line should have been more closely related to the build-up. For example, he could have "pulled the string" with: "That's funny," said the inmate. "I put sugar and cream on mine, and they've got me in the nut house!"

The improved phrasing more clearly points up the insanity angle. It doubles the laughter! Why? Because of man's inhumanity to man. The inmate thinks he's smarter than the farmer but that he's in the "booby-hatch" in spite of it. The improved phrasing brings this out more strongly.

The main point here: Build-up makes way for the punch line, gets the audience ready for it. Naturally, the build-up should establish the basis for the laugh—inhumanity, natural target, the unexpected, or sex. But the punch line should bear out this basis. Unless there's strong relationship between the build-up and the punch line, the story loses much of its sock.

### HOW TO FIND HUMOR FOR A TALK

Funny stories can be found everywhere.

You hear them from friends. You hear them on radio and

# HOW TO PUT *HUMOR* INTO A SPEECH

television programs. You can obtain books that are filled with jokes. You can even originate a funny story or two.*

"My best stories have been those I originated," declared an advertising executive in Milwaukee. "I think back to some amusing incident in which I was the goat. My next step is to see how very stupid I can make me appear. Then I tell it on myself. It always gets a hoot of glee."

A friend reported, "I was required to mention my wife in one particular speech and to tell of how she had helped me. I was afraid it would sound too lovey dovey.' So I threw in the following: 'You can see that ours is a happy marriage. But all marriages are happy, for that matter. It's the living together afterwards that caused all of our fights!'

"It pleased the audience for me to admit that I'd had a few battles with the wife. Why? Because of man's inhumanity to man."

When originating a joke, be sure to decide which of the four reasons the audience will have for laughing. Then make sure that your words and tone make the most of it.

## HOW TO RELATE HUMOR TO YOUR OTHER MATERIAL

The best humor is that related to the rest of your speech. Related stories are more natural and can help illustrate various parts of your talk.

For instance, a speaker was talking on the need for consumer acceptance of his product. He told this related story . . .

The sales manager for a dog food concern was holding a sales meeting. He started in an enthusiastic manner by yelling at his men, "Who's *got the best* dog food in *the* world?" The men yelled back in unison, "We have/"

"Who's got *the best* advertising and sales promotion program for *this* dog food?" The same answer was shouted back—"We have/"

"And who's got *the best sales* force to *sell this* dog *food?"* Again it came back—"We have/"

Whereupon, the sales manager said, "Let's face it men. If all this is true, why aren't we selling more dog food?"

---

* A good source book is *New* Treasury of Stories for Every Speaking and Writing Occasion, by Jacob M. Brande. (Englewood-Cliffs, N. J.: Prentice-Hall, Inc.).

*A* little fellow in the back row said, "I know why. It's simple—the darned dogs don't like it!"

Did he illustrate his point regarding the need for customer acceptance? You bet he did!

To relate humor to a speech, first prepare the speech. Don't build a talk around some jokes. Develop the speech, and *then* work in the humor.

Consider the point of your talk. What funny stories do you know on the same subject? How can they be adapted so that they will illustrate your point?

A joke needn't be told in exactly the same way that you heard it or read it. Change it to meet the needs of your speech.

Then go to the next part of your speech, the reasons for your point. Can a story or two be tied in there?

And how about your examples? Certainly some of the examples will offer an opportunity for related humor. Sometimes a joke can serve as the example itself. For instance, a speaker was talking on how to give good customer service. One of his examples was that the customer should not be overloaded with any one item. He told this story, which served as the example almost by itself:

"A grocer had gone broke. The receivers were taking an inventory. They found the store filled to the brim with bread. There was bread in the front and bread in the back. They found white bread, whole wheat bread, French bread, rye bread, potato bread, cracked wheat bread, Roman meal bread, and other kinds of bread!

"They remarked to the grocer, 'You surely sold a lot of bread, didn't you?'

" 'Oh, no,' he replied. 'But that fellow who calls on me from the bakery surely sells a lot of it!' "

### GO EASY ON THE PUNS

A pun is a play on words, words that have the same sound but a different meaning. Or a pun may involve different applications of a word.

A nightclub comic will use every wile to capture his audience,

# HOW *TO PUT HUMOR INTO A SPEECH*

even the lowly pun: "Our next number is entitled, 'Suffering In The Wigwams,' or 'Her Torture Was Intense!'" and "Or as one strawberry said to the other, 'If we hadn't been in the same bed together, we wouldn't be in this jam now.'"

The pun is sometimes referred to as the lowest form of humor. That's because it traps the listener. To some degree it makes *a* dupe of him.

A pun goes over best if related to the sentence preceding it. Regardless, it takes a very high degree of skill to use a pun effectively. Even the professional comedians often fall flat. Therefore, go easy on the puns.

### BE CAREFUL OF THE TENDENCY TO ASSOCIATE

A speaker might pop three or four funny stories in a row. This causes the audience to become more and more relaxed. People laugh harder when they've been put in a laughing mood.

But look out! When you leave the humor, the audience may snicker at something of a serious nature. That's because they're in a laughing mood—you've put them there. Thus, your transition to something more serious should be clearly understood.

For example, it could be prefaced with something like, "We can laugh all we want to. But seriously, folks . . ."

By bringing them back down to earth before getting serious, you avoid the embarrassment of people laughing in the wrong places.

There's also another tendency to associate. The tendency to associate actions and props with those previously used.

For instance, a speaker started his talk, while wearing an old looking hat. He cracked several jokes about it. Then he bridged into his point skillfully. And, as he became serious, he removed the hat.

Near the end he donned the hat again. This was a mistake. The audience associated it with the funny stories told earlier. They laughed just as he was restating his point with a plea for action. The result was a poor ending to an otherwise excellent speech.

So be certain that the serious sections of your speech are suf-

# HOW TO PUT HUMOR INTO A SPEECH

ficiently disassociated from the humor. A laugh in the wrong place makes the speaker look weak.

Additional tips on humor are contained in the chapter on "How To Emcee A Sales Meeting." Some vital suggestions can be found there.

**HOW TO PUT HUMOR IN A SPEECH**

How to Tell Stories Effectively

Use the Four Basic Platforms for Humor

Have a Double Barrel Appeal

Where to Find Funny Stories

How to Relate Humor to the Rest of Your Speech

Go Easy on the Pun Be Careful of the

Tendency to Associate

# 9. Forty-Five Ways to Put Life Into a Speech

---

A dynamic speaker "took the stand" at San Francisco's famous Cow Palace. He spoke on civil defense. With good organization of material, he held the audience spellbound. Nearly an hour later he still had the complete attention of an audience of thousands.

How did he do it? Was it organization of material alone? Or did his subject have an unusual appeal? Did he capitalize on basic emotions and urges?

### THE APPEAL TO BASIC EMOTIONS AND URGES

Indeed his subject had exceptional appeal. It encompassed the first law of human nature, the first human instinct—self-preservation! As he progressed, he also appealed to love of family, love of fellow men, love of country, and love of God. Further, he stimulated one of the most powerful of all human emotions-fear!

The most convincing speeches are usually like that one. They're directed at basic emotions and urges. A spark already burns in the heart of the audience. The speaker needs only to fan the flame.

Such flames should be fanned when the opportunity presents itself, but the speaker at a sales meeting has little opportunity to appeal to emotions and urges. Systems and procedures are without emotion. Besides, it's the prospective customer, not the salesman, whose emotions must usually be considered.

## HOW TO IMPROVE YOUR SPEAKERS AND SPEECHES

Yet, there's a means of putting sparkle in speeches at sales meetings. That means is showmanship. *Speakers should dramatize their speeches, present them in a vivid manner, illustrate them visually, and bring them to life.*

The presentation of each participant can be previewed to determine whether enough life has been injected. Speeches, particularly, should be checked. Where more showmanship is needed, it can be added.

### How to Put Sparkle in Speakers and Speeches

1. *To dramatize the qualities necessary for success in selling,* your speaker could *actually erect a miniature log cabin.* "Here's the bottom log. It represents a desire to serve others, which is the foundation of good salesmanship. Unless the salesman and his product will serve the customers in some way, there's little basis for a sale. On top of that log we place the next, which represents enthusiasm. A good salesman has enthusiasm for people and enthusiasm for his product. The next log is knowledge of the product. We must know what we are selling . . ."

Miniature log cabins can be purchased at toy shops. The logs need be only ten or twelve inches long but grooved so they will interlock. The roof is placed on last. It should represent a protective element, such as a code of ethics or a manufacturer's guarantee.

2. *Perhaps you want your salesmen to be better sold on their own proposition.* If so, assign someone the subject, "My Most Difficult Prospect."

Your speaker begins by stating that he once had a very tough prospect. After elaborating on how tough he was, the speaker passes out "pictures" of him. Each "picture" proves to be a small mirror.

"Yes, there's the most difficult prospect you've ever met. If you sell him on your product line, and if you keep him sold, you can sell your merchandise to anyone on the face of the earth! Let's

## *PUTTING LIFE* INTO A SPEECH

discuss the many reasons why we should be sold on our merchandise. . ."

#### HOW TO ADD SHOWMANSHIP TO ANY TALK

3. *Showmanship can* be added *to any talk by* any speaker. For example, let's assume your speaker has a subject that is drab. Let's also assume he has examples of how the thing works. He could use balloons in presenting his examples. Thin, sausage-shaped balloons can be inflated. One is rubbed briskly on any clothing. Static electricity is created. The balloon is then placed against a wall. Surprisingly enough, it will stay there. Your speaker could paint the key word in each example on one of the balloons. As an example is developed, he rubs the appropriate balloon against his hip and places it "on" the wall.

4. Props can help tell *the* story. When telling of a trip, the speaker holds up a suitcase. To represent a baby, he picks up a doll. While mentioning golf, he brandishes a mashie.

To show he'd been dumb, your speaker puts on a dunce cap. Smart—a graduation mortarboard. Sleep—a night cap. Fishing—a sloppy felt. Bad weather—a rain cap.

A hat that's much too small can be donned to illustrate a sales presentation that's too brief. A hat that's much too large—a sales talk that's too long. Point: a good sales talk fits the prospect.

5. *Sometimes a* speaker *will talk on balance.* It may be a balance between selling the need for his product and selling the product itself. Or it may be the balance between selling the customer and servicing him. Regardless, it would be appropriate to show an old fashioned balance scale. It can be used to excellent advantage in making the point.

6. Suppose someone were speaking on "The Road To Success." He could use realism; signs of the proper color, size, and shape could be improvised.

A STOP sign is shown. "It's the thing to do when you're about to argue with a customer. STOP!"

A DANGER sign is shown. "When asked to cut the price-look out! There's danger in price cutting."

# 94  *PUTTING LIFE INTO A SPEECH*

*A* DETOUR sign is shown. "When asked for an item you don't have, make a detour. Suggest the nearest thing to it that will meet your prospect's need."

Signs saying SLOW, CURVE, SCHOOL, BRIDGE, DEAD END, and WASH OUT are easily adaptable.

**HOW TO USE COSTUMING**

7. When one *of* your speakers appears *in costume,* color *is added.* The theme of the meeting will usually suggest costuming ideas.

Case in point: The National Society of Sales Training Executives used "Five Ring Circus" as the theme for a meeting. The emcee was dressed like a ring master. One speaker was attired as a tight-rope-walker, another as a clown. Still another displayed the costume and muscles of a circus strong man.

8. *Costuming can often be connected with the subject ofi the speech.* "The Art of Selling" might be the subject. The speaker appears as an artist. He wears a smock and tarn, possibly with a thin mustache. He carries a brush and palette. Thus he "paints" a vivid, visual picture and he can actually paint his major points on a canvas mounted on a tripod.

9. *Even a talk on selling as a career can be spiced.* Your speaker appears in work clothes of his prior occupation. If he was a brakeman on a railroad, he makes his talk while wearing the same over alls he wore before. A denim cap, red bandana, and brakeman's lantern would complete the costuming. He connects his unusual attire by telling how and why he left a brakeman's job to become a salesman.

**HOW TO AAAKE A TALK LIGHT AND INTERESTING**

10. A *talk on courtesy to the customer could be very boring.* But here's how your speaker can put animation in it. He stages a demonstration. "Now we'll enact a scene involving customer courtesy. This incident takes place in a grocery store. I'll play the

## PUTTING LIFE INTO A SPEECH 95

part of the customer. Fred Jones, approaching the speakers' stand dressed as a grocer, will act as the salesman." The customer asks three or four questions about the merchandise: "Where is the flour? Are these the best potatoes you have? Don't you have cheaper tomatoes?" The clerk is indifferent, then discourteous, then extremely rude. The climax is reached when the customer angrily declares, "If that's the way you treat your customers, you can take your groceries and go to the devil!" The customer throws several grocery items, including a sack of flour, at the retreating clerk. The sack hits the wall. A hole in it causes flour to be strewn in all directions! Your audience will roar. They'll then be receptive to your speaker's remarks on the subject.

11. A "dry run" *given by* one of your speakers may *show that he's planning to* "preach" to *his audience.* If so, something should be done about it. An audience doesn't like to be told, "You gotta do this and you gotta do that."

Your speaker could animate his speech by introducing a "prospective customer" to the audience. He asks the "prospect" why he bought from another company. The "prospect" refuses to reveal anything except that he was given a better deal.

Then the speaker "hypnotizes" the "prospect." When quizzed under "hypnosis" the "prospect" tells the truth. "I really wanted to buy from Johnny Jones—that salesman (he points to the audience) sitting there. But he gave up too soon. If he doesn't sell on the first try, he gives up." The "prospect" continues, using points the speaker had originally planned to use in his talk. "And I couldn't buy from Ed Smith, because he doesn't know his merchandise. As for Charley Brown, he always wants to argue!"

12. *Here's* another way to accomplish *the same thing.* Your speaker can lighten his presentation by using a hand puppet—the type worn like a glove. The puppet brings out the main ideas, the speaker confirming them. The speaker can operate the puppet himself. Since he's not likely to be a ventriloquist, he could play a tape recording for the voice of the puppet. Better still, there can be a second person concealed from view. He operates the puppet and serves as its voice.

## HOW TO COVER BASIC FUNDAMENTALS EFFECTIVELY

13. A speaker can *easily fall Bat if he talks about personal habits.* As one salesman said, "Any time I want to hear a sermon I'll go to church!" Yet, habits such as smoking, drinking and gum chewing must sometimes be covered. Here's how the talk can be made interesting and effective.

A member of the audience is called forward to act as the prospect. Your speaker acts as the salesman. The speaker takes a couple of quick drinks from a bottle marked "Old Red Eye." He then simulates a sales call on the prospect. The latter appears to choke on the speaker's breath!

Then the speaker unwraps a whole package of chewing gum and crams it into his mouth. His "sales presentation" becomes very hard to understand. Next, he lights a tremendous cigar and blows a cloud of smoke at his prospect's face!

Now the audience is loose and receptive. The speaker can end the skit and put across his ideas on personal habits.

14. A *talk on customer service is likely to "go in one ear and out the other."* After all, most salesmen have heard it many times before. A fresh approach is needed. For example, your speaker can explain the origin of a "baker's dozen."

"Little Willie went five blocks out of his way each time his mother sent him to the bakery. Why? Because the baker would count out the twelve doughnuts Willie requested. Then he'd give Willie an extra to eat on the way home."

The point, service, should then be applied to your own method of selling. The story can be climaxed by passing out doughnuts. A break for coffee might logically follow.

15. *Or service to customers can be dramatized in the following way:* The speaker shows a jar of dried beans. He says, "Each bean represents a customer. These little customers look very much alike, don't they? Yet, each is different from the rest. And since every customer is different, each wants different treatment and service. Give each exactly what he wants.

"I found exactly what one of these little customers wanted.

# PUTTING LIFE INTO A SPEECH

Then I gave it to him. I'll show you what happened." The speaker reveals a long green vine—visual evidence that a customer "blooms" when given the treatment he wants. The audience will then be receptive to a few words on customer service.

16. Salesmen *should like* people. When this point is covered at a sales meeting, however, it's usually to no avail. The idea is too general for specific results. The next time one of your speakers is slated to cover this point, he can be introduced this way: "Write down the names of three people whom you like. These three people can be friends, acquaintances, relatives, in-laws, outlaws—anybody."

"All through? Next, delete the names of those who, in your opinion, do not like you. All done? Now let's see the hand of everyone who deleted one or more names." Probably not a single hand will be raised.

"This shows that the people you like, are the people who like you. Like, to be liked!"

### HOW TO DRAMATIZE MENTAL ATTITUDE

17. Mental *attitude is intangible.* As insurance and securities salesmen know, it's difficult to present an intangible in a dramatic way. It's difficult to present it at all. It can't even be seen!

But here's how to dramatize mental attitude. Your speaker shows a 10-foot plank, 2 inches thick and 4 inches wide. He places it on the floor and has two or three volunteers walk the length of it.

Then he states that the board will be placed on the tops of two adjacent buildings, each five stories high. It will connect the roofs of the two structures. Who will volunteer to walk it? No one.

"Everyone can do it. At least, he can when the plank is on the floor. When it's high, you're afraid you'll fall. And that fear would likely cause your downfall, too."

The point is then applied to selling. Where one is confident he will make a sale, he may make it. When he fears failure, he will experience it.

18. Here's another way *the same thing* can be demonstrated.

# PUTTING LIFE INTO A SPEECH

Your speaker distributes shiny new tin cans. In each can there's a slip of paper on which the word "Success" has been written. He proves, then, that success comes in cans—not can'ts.

19. *Good mental attitude includes a willingness to look for the good instead of the bad.* This willingness can also be dramatized. Your speaker gets a large white poster and places a small black circle near the center. During his talk he holds up the poster and asks, "What do you see?" The reply will be, "A black dot." Then he "lowers the boom" on them. "Here's a fine white poster. It has quality and distinction. It can be used for many things. You could print directions on it and use it in routing customer traffic. You could print merchandise information on it and use it in sales promotion.

"But you didn't visualize those things. You didn't see the good. All you saw was the one little blemish—the bad!

"Let's start looking for the good in everything. It's a cinch we can't benefit from the bad!"

20. *Here's the same "song" but a different "verse."* Your speaker can show a glass of water that's half full. He states, "The negative thinker will say the glass is half empty. The positive thinker will say it's half full. Which way do you think?"

**HOW TO BRING THE LAW OF AVERAGES TO LIFE**

21. "See *enough people, and you'll do your share oi the selling.* The law of averages will take care of you." This idea has been covered time and time again. It's a basic truth, too. Outside sales men should lean heavily on the law of averages. But the idea soon becomes "old hat." Your speaker must enliven it in some way if he's to get results. He can do it this way . . .

When he starts his talk, he shakes up a 1,000 pennies and throws them on a table. The table is then taken out of the room and the speech begun. The climax is reached when the speaker announces, "I've told you the law of averages is infallible. Now you'll see that it actually is."

A slip of paper is handed to him. "While I've been talking, four men have been in the next room counting pennies. They counted

## PUTTING LIFE INTO A SPEECH

the number that turned up heads, and the number that turned up tails. Here's their report . . . Of the 1,000 pennies, exactly 501 turned up heads and 499 showed tails. There's proof positive that the law of averages will work. Put it to work for you!"

22. *The law* of averages *is sometimes* expressed *this* way—"See enough prospects and you'll get enough customers." But how can your speaker dramatize it?

He can get a large clear glass jar. He partially fills it with dried red beans. Then he puts in three ping pong balls. More beans are used to complete the filling. It's important that the balls are not adjacent to the glass—only the beans should be visible. Your speaker explains, "Each bean represents a prospect. Let's see what happens when you 'mix it up' with a lot of prospects." He shakes the jar vigorously. Because ping pong balls are lighter than the beans, they work their way to the top. As each ball appears on the top, the speaker makes a comment such as, "And out of those prospects, up pops a customer. Action pays off. See enough prospects, and you'll make enough sales."

**HOW TO DRAMATIZE SYSTEMATIC PROSPECTING**

23. Here's an effective way your speaker can *dramatize "see the people."*

The speaker begins by holding up a large comb that has several missing teeth. He asks the audience what it represents. Answer: high spotting—hitting the high spots of a territory. Why and how to "comb" a territory thoroughly is then explained. The speaker closes on a high note by passing out pocket combs. Each comb has been imprinted with the words "Your Territory." Thus the men will carry constant reminders to see people, to "comb" their territories.

24. *Here's the same point, made in a different way.*

Your speaker is dressed as a magician. He begins by performing several magic tricks. Three people are then brought forward. They should be strangers to the audience. One is said to be a hot prospect, ready to place an order. Your speaker guesses which of the three it is. He misses on his first guess—on the second one, too.

"This proves that no one can tell which prospects will buy—not even a magician. So let's call on everybody."

**HOW TO PRESENT THE CUSTOMER'S POINT OF VIEW**

25. Salespeople must constantly be r*eminded that the customer's point of view is* different. Here's how your speaker can show that difference in viewpoint. He distributes thin pieces of paper (Onion skin, 81/2" by 11", is ideal) and tells the audience: "Fold a sheet in half and tear a little out of the center. Now fold again and tear a small section out of the side. Fold once more, tear a bit of the left corner. Now open your sheets and compare them."

No two will be alike. Some will be far different from others. "You started with the same type of paper. Each sheet was the same size. Everyone was given the same instructions, too. Yet the results are quite different. That's because the instructions meant different things to different people. No viewpoints are ever the same. And so it is with a customer. His viewpoint is different from yours."

26. Your speaker *might better illustrate the point by stepping out of his shoes while speaking.* He ties the laces together and puts the shoes around his neck. "I'm not wearing my shoes now. A good salesman never does. He steps into his customer's shoes. He sees things from his customer's viewpoint."

**HOW TO SHOW LOSS OR GAIN**

27. *Here's* a sure fire *method of appealing to the fear of loss.* Your speaker flips a silver dollar in the air three or four times while speaking. He catches it each time, saying nothing about it. At the proper moment he tosses it out an open window and says, "That's what's happening. You're throwing money away!"

28. *The desire of gain can also be stimulated by demonstration.* The speaker places a covered table next to the rostrum. Under the cover is a ham, turkey, a pair of men's shoes, a lady's hat, and other desirable items. He recommends use of a certain principle. "It will bring each salesman an increase in earnings of $50 per

# PUTTING LIFE INTO A SPEECH

month." Then he yanks the cover off the table. The audience actually sees the monthly benefit!

## HOW TO ACT OUT VARIOUS POINTS

29. *There's no excuse for a boring speech when your speakers can act out ANY POINT.* This applies even to a code of ethics. It seems pretty dull. How could adherence to a code of ethics be dramatized?

Your speaker simply extends a long stick toward an assistant. He nearly touches him before withdrawing the stick. He repeats the act. Then the assistant says, "I know you need me. And I can really sell." But the speaker gives a negative shake of his head.

The assistant drops to his knees with a plea of, "Please! Please take me!" The speaker tosses the stick away, explaining to the audience, "He won't adhere to the code of ethics. I wouldn't touch him with a ten-foot pole!"

30. *The need for having a goal plan can easily be enacted.* Your speaker appoints someone to play the role of a salesman. "This salesman has set a goal for himself and is trying to reach it. This check for $30,000 represents his goal."

The salesman is asked to leave the room for a moment. While he's gone the check is taped high on the wall in the rear of the room. He's called back in and told to "take whatever steps he must take in order to reach his goal."

He wanders about, looking in many places. He may even look down the collar of the big boss! But he fails to find the check, fails to reach his goal.

Speaker: "He had a goal but no plan for reaching it. Break your goal down into small steps. Then you'll know what must be done each day in order to reach it. A goal, without a plan for reaching it, is merely wishful thinking."

## HOW TO MAKE YOUR SPEAKERS GET HOT

31. Many *speakers should be jabbed with a red hot pole.* They're too dull! While a good sales manager won't use a poker, he will do other things. For instance, he might pick out two or three

places where emphasis is needed. He asks the speaker to pound the podium at those points in his talk. The pounding is practiced. This loosens up the speaker and causes him to put more life in *all* of his talk.

Or a pitcher of water and a glass can be placed on the stand. He knocks them off at the climax of his talk. An enthusiastic sweep of his arm, in a natural way, will give the audience something to remember!

32. For a talk *on enthusiasm,* your speaker must be a sparkling example. He could say, "If you are really enthusiastic, people will be grabbing at your coat tail to get in on this thing you're so hepped-up about. They'll literally rip your coat wide open!" At this moment he tears off half his coat!

He continues with, "Nothing can cool off an enthusiastic salesman. Not even a pitcher of ice water poured on the top of his head." He promptly empties a pitcher of water over his own head!

33. If your speaker *is incapable ofi getting hot, the audience can help.* Occasionally, someone must be used as a speaker regardless of his temperature. When all else fails, the audience can help him. He could offer a prize for the best answer submitted in writing on subject concerned.

As an example, he might be speaking on product information. He can offer a prize to the person giving the best 25 words on "What I like most about my merchandise." Time is allowed so answers can be written during the meeting. This minimizes his speaking.

Judging takes place in another room while the meeting progresses. Near the end of the meeting a few of the best answers are read and briefly discussed. The prize is then awarded.

The contest won't make the speaker any hotter. But it will make his part of the meeting more enjoyable. Your sales force will derive more benefit, too.

### HOW TO ARRANGE TIMELY INTERRUPTIONS

34. A dry speech *will be* more interesting *ii* interruptions are planned. It might be a talk on advertising, for instance. The

# PUTTING LIFE INTO A SPEECH

speaker leads up to his point with questions such as, "What makes it easy to sell our goods? What is it that softens buyer resistance everywhere?" Someone in the rear of the room yells, "Advertising!" The surprise interruption stimulates the audience and helps make the point that advertising is productive.

35. Or your speaker can plan *it this way* . . . After a couple of minutes of generalities, a member of the audience rises to leave. The speech is stopped while the speaker asks the fellow for an explanation. The man says, "I'm leaving. You're not speaking on anything important. I had hoped to hear about the salesman's best friend."

"What do you mean? What's the salesman's best friend?" Then the fellow yells, "Advertising!" A speech on that subject promptly follows.

36. *It's effective to enact* a *point by means of* interruptions. For example, a janitor suddenly appears and starts mopping the floor near the speakers' stand. The speaker asks him to leave, but the janitor continues mopping.

Finally the janitor explains, "My orders are to mop the floor. And orders are orders. When I'm told to do something, I do it. I do it promptly, and I do it well. And I don't let some character like you stop me! I've finished mopping now, so I'll leave."

The speaker covers the point just enacted. "When given a job to do, do it. Be like the janitor. Let nothing side-track you."

37. Another *twist* . . . "Some of you aren't working. Just as sure as I have on a necktie, some of you are loafing on the job." A member of the audience dashes from the rear of the room with a pair of scissors. He snips off the speaker's tie!

"As I was saying, just as sure as I'm wearing a necktie . . . And, I'm not wearing one. You've been doing anything but loafing. I want to congratulate you on your hustle and spirit."

## HOW TO ANIMATE SPEECHES WITH CROSSOVERS

38. *The audience likes to see any idea* presented *by a* speaker. A visual presentation can be made at the same time as the verbal. And it can be made in several different ways.

# 104        PUTTING LIFE INTO A SPEECH

*A* good method is the crossover, an individual crossing the platform behind the speaker. The person crossing can illustrate many things with real effectiveness.

39. *Suppose the speaker wants to tell of an* overconfident sales man. "He vowed he'd eat his hat if he couldn't sell a certain pros pect." This is a natural for a crossover! When the climax of the story is reached, a fellow crosses the stage chewing on his hat!

40. Perhaps *the speaker refers to a fellow who became a smart alec—"too* big for his britches." Someone with the seat torn out of his trousers could crossover.

41. "He *lost!*[7] said the speaker. "He almost lost his shirt." A fellow in an undershirt (and trousers) could then crossover.

42. *"This man made a million dollars." A* fellow crosses with money sticking out of every pocket, and pinned to his shoulders and back. He's smoking a long cigar and counting some bills in his hands.

43. "That *competition of ours really took* a *beating."* The cross over is made by a man who has a bandaged eye, an arm in a sling, and catsup on his cheek!

### WHEN TO HAVE YOUR SPEAKERS DESTROY THEIR NOTES

44. A *few sales executives boast that notes aren't needed.* Most speak better however, when using notes. Except for the "pros," all speakers should use notes. Even a "pro" uses them until he has his talk down "pat." There are times when your speaker can destroy his notes with effectiveness, however.

First, he might do it for the sake of informality. Upon taking the stand he looks at his audience and states, "I see Bill Lawson, Plasco Moore and other friends in the audience." He rips up his notes with a flourish, adding, "And I certainly don't need notes to talk to my friends." Although the audience doesn't realize it, he may still have a few notes before him!

45. *There's another time for note tearing.* It's when a meeting is behind schedule and the audience is aware of it. The final speaker begins with a glance at his watch and a fast rate of speech. "We're running out of time, so here goes the advice I'd planned

to give you." He then tears a blank piece of paper down the middle. The audience giggles with relief.

"And here go the funny stories I'd planned to tell!" He rips some more paper. The audience relaxes and laughs louder. He captured full attention in spite of a difficult situation. Everyone is listening when he adds, "There's only one part of the talk I'll go through with, the part you wanted most to hear. I'm referring to ____ "

### PUTTING LIFE INTO A SPEECH

**Capitalize on Basic Emotions and Urges**

**Suggest Showmanship To Your Speakers**

—Props—

—Costuming—

—Skits—

—Demonstrations—

—Dramatizations—

# 10.  How to Make Good Physical Arrangements

It doesn't take a wizard to make good physical arrangements. "Horse sense" is ample. Take location of the meeting room, for example. You may have a suitable room at your office, store, or plant. If so, use it. "Our sales meetings are always conducted on the premises," declared a Pittsburg industrialist. "The various things we need for the meeting are readily available here. Then, too, our salesmen must come to the plant anyway to confer with members of the staff, make reports and pick up supplies. We didn't have a large meeting room, so we built one. It has proved to be an excellent investment."

In some instances the audience will arrive from distant points and an overnight stay is necessary. Put all of them up at the same hotel, then conduct your meeting there. If a trip to your plant is desired, busses can be chartered. "We favor hotel meetings," said an Omaha sales manager. "Nearly all of our men are called in from out of town. Since they're staying at a hotel, it's easier for us to hold our meetings there and avoid confusion."

Only you can decide the best locale for your meeting. Select a place that is convenient for all the people attending, and one that is practical and within budget limitations.

**HOW TO LOCATE DESIRABLE MEETING ROOMS**

The best public meeting rooms are booked a year or more in advance, especially in the case of large auditoriums and ballrooms. Do some long range planning.

## HOW TO MAKE PHYSICAL ARRANGEMENTS 107

"I represent a group of fashion exhibitors," said a New York man. "We do shows all over the country. The competition for the best ballrooms is so great that I've booked five years ahead in several cities. It's the only way I can be sure of getting the hotel I want."

You may need help in finding a desirable downtown meeting place. Contact the Chamber of Commerce, their staff will know of many suitable rooms.

A United States Chamber of Commerce official reports, "Most Chambers keep a roster of available meeting rooms. In addition to the location of each room, the local Chamber can tell you the capacity, the cost and the name of the person to contact. You can obtain this information whether your company belongs to the local Chamber or not."

Gratis rooms can be booked in some cities. In addition to the Chamber, check the public library, Y.M.C.A., Y.W.C.A., public utility auditoriums, and public school facilities, where a clean-up fee is often the only change. Another means of getting a free meeting room is to schedule a meal. Most hotels charge only for food-breakfast, lunch or dinner. *Nothing* is actually free. In paying for the food, you also pay for the room. This hidden cost is usually quite reasonable, however. It's most economical when food activities include a meal other than dinner. The trend is to charge heavily for dinner. "They'll really soak you for an evening meal," said a vending-machine operator. "Ask whether a less expensive meal is available. Usually they push the higher priced meal, but most hotels will serve a substantial lunch for a buck or two less."

### HOW TO ARRANGE FOR MEALS

Plan conventional meals and avoid exotic dishes. This way you'll please nearly everybody. Never cater to the gourmets. Strive to satisfy Mr. Average Salesman. "The last time we had a 'blowout' we arranged for Cornish game-hens," said a Newark man. "We later learned that most of the men wanted steaks even though the steaks were less expensive. And even though *they'd been* eating steaks at nearly every meal." So give them what they want, not what they should want.

# 108  HOW TO MAKE PHYSICAL ARRANGEMENTS

Is your meeting on Friday? If so, some will want fish. How about ham—anyone object?

You must pay for the number of plates guaranteed or the number of plates served—whichever is greater. This is standard procedure. Experience has shown that a few people miss organized meals. There's always someone who can't kick himself out of bed in time for breakfast. Another can't tear himself loose from the bar at noon. Two more excuse themselves before dinner so they can "do the town." One gets sick. Still another is called home by an emergency. Why guarantee that everyone will show for every meal? Reduce the guarantee figure by 8 or 10 percent. You'll save money. You won't have to pay for food that "goes begging."

If everyone does happen to show, there's no harm done. The hotel will be prepared to serve 10 percent more than the number guaranteed. This also is standard procedure.

### How to Choose the Best Meeting Room

The best room is a little longer than wide and has no columns to block vision and segregate the audience. "The architects who design columns in meeting rooms should have to sit behind them," a salesman ruefully declared. "It's no fun."

The ceiling should be high enough that visuals can be shown to good advantage. If a chandelier is in the way, perhaps it can be removed. Inquire and see.

Low ceilings are also to be avoided since they tend to depress an audience. "I feel boxed in," is the way one fellow expressed it. "It's not so bad at first, but it gets 'old' real quick! As the day progresses you get a worried feeling. There's no relief until you leave the room. It's as bad as being on a crowded elevator."

Use a room that has entrances and exits in the rear. Reason: late arrivals and early departures will not be so distracting.

Naturally, the room should be large enough. But it should also be small enough—small enough that it's comfortably filled. Vacant space and empty chairs are deadly.

Dressing room screens can be used to reduce the meeting area. It's better, though, to select a room of the right size in the first

# HOW TO MAKE PHYSICAL ARRANGEMENTS 109

place. "I'd rather have a few people standing than a lot of empty chairs/' said an advertising account executive. "It leaves the impression the meeting is so important that everyone wants to get in on it."

## BE CERTAIN TO INSPECT THE ROOM

Physical arrangements are a "snap" for those who can use the same room all the time. But when a different room will be used, inspect it. Even if it's in the next county, inspect it. See it before publicizing the meeting. You may want to change rooms.

Perhaps you've used the room before. If you haven't seen it in the past year, inspect it anyway. This especially applies to hotel rooms, which are remodeled continually. The Sierra Room may be half the size this year, or it may be three times as large. Names are changed, too. This year's Sierra Room may be what you remember as the Keystone Room. "I learned my lesson the hard way," said a Las Vegas business man. "They had remodeled an adjacent room for a dance studio. Had I inspected the facilities, I would have known that their music would interfere with our sales meeting."

## PROS AND CONS OF SEATING ARRANGEMENTS

The best room is one in which you can arrange the best seating. Therefore, your selection of a room should be based, in part, on seating arrangements.

There are four basic types of seating:

1. Auditorium style. This arrangement is most widely used. It consists simply of one row of chairs behind another, as in a movie house. "We've always favored the auditorium style," said a Denver retailer. "It enables us to get the greatest number of people in the room. You see, tables take up space—more space than people." Auditorium style is okay for meetings lasting a couple of hours or less. For longer meetings, however, this arrangement is tiring. People want tables on which to lean and to keep cigarettes. Be sure to stagger the chairs. The guy in front may not be thick headed, but . . .

2. Conference style. Each person is seated at a table. The

table is shaped like an I, a T, or a U. This is ideal for note taking, water pouring, elbow resting, and the like. It's comfortable. "Conference style is best for creating informality," said a building supply executive. "To get group discussion, you can't beat it."

Tables consume so much space that conference style is used only for smaller meetings. However, it's the smaller meeting that's best for group discussion.

3. *Spotted Tables.* Small tables are spotted at certain places in the room. From two to eight people are seated at each table. This requires extra floor space. In fact, it's a good means of trimming a large room to the size needed. It's also practical when the audience is to be divided into small groups, as in buzz sessions.

An educational leader said, "In some of our meetings we assign different projects to different groups of people. Each group works on its project then and there—right in the meeting room. Spotted tables are ideal for this. A different project can be assigned to the people at each table. A natural division of the audience is provided."

4. *Theater in the* round. You've seen this seating arrangement at boxing and wrestling matches. The stage is surrounded by seats. The average spectator is closer to the action. Some seats are a third nearer the stage. There's more realism, too—a better 3-D effect. But it's a poor arrangement for the average sales meeting. A speaker's stand cannot be used since it would face only a small part of the audience. Participants feel naked.

Speakers must turn constantly to make eye contact with all the audience. If the crowd is so large that a p.a. system is used, a portable mike is necessary. As speakers walk, the wire to the mike is twisted. Sooner or later, action must be stopped while the cord is unwound. Some "character" finally trips on the cord! And it's difficult to use visuals. Films are out of the question. Generated charts and chalk boards, too. A visual must be used in such a way that everyone can see it. Either it has four faces, or it's turned completely around by the speaker. Both are clumsy.

"I'll never forget the first time I spoke at a meeting arranged like a theater in the round. It was very confusing. I couldn't decide on which part of the audience to concentrate. I was never so un-

# HOW TO MAKE PHYSICAL ARRANGEMENTS 111

comfortable before people. I felt that I was on public display." Who told this sad story? A talented public speaker. So beware of theater in the round.

Be sure to select a room that permits the seating arrangement you consider best.

## POOR ACOUSTICS ARE MURDER!

Before booking a room, check the acoustics. If voices of your participants bounce around, you're in for trouble. A speaker can't be understood when acoustics are bad. He can be heard, but not clearly heard. It's exasperating!

Sound engineering has made rapid strides in the last few years. But in the past there have been many instances when new ceilings had to be installed in new buildings. Why? The acoustics were poor.

Acoustics cannot be checked in the absence of an audience. The bodies of the people attending will alter the travel and effect of sound. Visit the room while a meeting is in progress. If this isn't practical, contact someone who booked a recent meeting there. If acoustics were bad, he will still be complaining about it!

## GUARD AGAINST ALIEN NOISES

Few rooms are soundproof. Inquire about activities to take place nearby. Will barbershop quartets turn up in the next room? Will an orchestra rehearse across the hall? Is noisy remodeling scheduled? How about noises from the outside? Is the street only a few stories below? Is it heavily traveled? Will there be open windows on warm days, or air conditioning?

## ANTICIPATE ALL PHYSICAL NEEDS BEFORE SELECTING A ROOM

Does the room have a stage? If not, can a platform be erected?

Is there a backstage area for hiding people? If not, can screens be used?

Will the building management permit company personnel to move props? If not, will union stagehands be available?

# 112 HOW TO MAKE PHYSICAL ARRANGEMENTS

Are rest room facilities adequate? If not, can additional facilities be used?

Will cloak room services be fast enough? If not, will self-service avoid a bottleneck?

Can telephones be removed? If not, can they be blocked by the switchboard operator?

Is a freight elevator available? If not, will doors, halls and stairways permit movement of bulky props?

Is the right type of current (AC or DC) available? If not, can the building engineer convert to what you need?

Does the engineer know whether your equipment will overload the line? If not, will the electric company advise you?

Is a p.a. system available? If not, will one be needed?

How about decorations? Are they needed?

Will a company banner or product display make the room look better?

### How to Select the Best "Mike" for Your Purpose

A good p.a. system must be strong and clear enough to command attention. The only way to tell whether a p.a. system is this good, is to listen to it when the room is filled with people.

The fellow who arranges a sales meeting will usually accept whatever p.a. equipment he's offered. He's safe in doing this most of the time, but occasionally he won't be offered the equipment that's best for his purpose. And every sales meeting is important enough that the proper equipment should be used. There are systems and there are other systems. The difference is much in the microphone of which there are three kinds: a one-directional, a two-directional, and an all-directional.

**THE ONE-DIRECTIONAL "MIKE" IS MOST POPULAR**

The first, the one-directional "mike," accepts sound from one side only. It's ideal for a permanent installation. This is the "mike" ordinarily used for speakers' stands. It picks up less noise from the audience since it accepts sound from the opposite side only. Be-

# HOW TO MAKE PHYSICAL ARRANGEMENTS 113

cause it's more sensitive in this one direction, the speaker need not be "glued" to it. He can move around. This freedom is very desirable, too. For words to become natural, their sound waves must travel a foot or more. With a one-directional "mike," the speaker can stand at least two feet away, which is an ideal distance. "I like to move around when speaking," said a Cincinnati sales promoter. "This helps me keep attention. Also, it's almost impossible to use visuals without moving around a little. Therefore, I prefer a one-directional "mike."

Use the one-directional "mike" for regular speaking functions. It offers fewer technical problems. There's less whistling and squealing, known as feedback.

### ADVANTAGES IN USING A TWO-DIRECTIONAL "MIKE"

The two-directional "mike" accepts sound equally well from front or back and is best for interviews, skits, or demonstrations where two participants face each other with the "mike" placed between them.

In some respects it is inferior to a one-directional "mike." But it's superior to the all-directional "mike" in these respects:

1. Refusing "outside" noises.
2. Giving the speaker freedom of movement.
3. Producing fewer technical difficulties.

### MINIMIZE USE OF THE ALL-DIRECTIONAL "MIKE"

The all-directional "mike" accepts sound from any direction. You often see this type of equipment on T.V. When a performer goes into the audience to interview someone, he usually carries an all-directional. This "mike" is the most versatile of all. It can be carried, hung around the neck, placed on a floor stand, or used on a table. Because it's so versatile, the all-directional is often purchased, as the one "mike" that will serve all the many uses. So you get an all-directional in spite of the fact that it does not serve these many uses in the best possible manner. Who suffers? You do! Leave the all-directional to the "pros." It's notorious for feedback and has caused trouble at many sales meetings. The "pro" has a sound control system and sound engineers. You don't.

Request the "mike" that is best for your purpose, minimizing use of the all-directional.

### Last Minute Details to Check

1. Get to the meeting room early. Then look around.
2. Check to see if the proper "mike" is installed. Test it.
3. A light behind the speakers' stand is tiring. If there's one there, turn it off.
4. Put room temperature 5 degrees below normal. The audience will raise it with body heat.
5. How about water, ash trays, pencils, scratch pads?
6. Find the engineer. Have him stand by in case the p.a. system gives trouble.
7. If there's to be registration at the door, move it outside-well away. It will be noisy. And assign someone to see that registration doesn't result in a bottleneck.

That's all there is to it. Go on. Have your meeting!

### HOW TO MAKE GOOD PHYSICAL ARRANGEMENTS

Look for the *Best* Meeting Room

Arrange Conventional Meals

Inspect the Room Yourself

Decide on the Best Seating Arrangement

Guard Against Alien Noises

Anticipate All Physical Needs

Request the "Mike" That Fits Your Needs

Check Last Minute Details

# 11. How to Ensure a Good Audience

Negative thoughts tend to close the mind. Because of this, an audience in a negative mood will ignore the material being presented. A Kentucky jeweler said, "We make it a point to keep sales meetings in a positive vein. Discussions of an objectionable nature are thereby prevented. It kills a meeting for someone to complain about whether a product can be sold or whether the price is too high. We'd be better off without such a meeting. We keep it positive from start to finish. This makes a better audience and a better meeting."

### HOW TO PUT SALES MEETINGS ON A POSITIVE PLANE

Where previous meetings always have been lively and interesting, a more positive atmosphere will automatically prevail. If the people were pleased before, they expect they'll be pleased now. But, regardless of previous meetings, several things can be done to assure a positive atmosphere.

In the first place, each meeting should be announced as if it will be a *joy* to attend—not a drudgery. The sales staff would like to think that a little fun will take place.

One company official went even further by setting up a small booth, similar to a check booth, near the entrance of the meeting room. A sign over the booth stated boldly, "Check Your Negative Thoughts Here." Persons entering got a laugh from it, and at the same time, however, were gently reminded that the meeting was not a session for airing petty gripes. "It worked pretty well," he said. 'The two or three people who normally give a little trouble were quiet as church-mice. Try it."

**HOW TO USE THE MAGIC OF MUSIC**

Recorded music, played for several minutes before the meeting, helps set the proper mood. Peppy numbers are best. Many firms use military marches, while others play music connected with the theme. If you are staging a large meeting, connect the recorder with the p.a. system. Whether you use a record player or a tape recorder, better equipment will enable you to do this. It has the necessary mechanical features, and the result is better amplification.

Be certain to consider this effective means of setting a healthy mood. The results will far exceed the effort involved. You'll likely find it helpful in sustaining the mood, too. Try it during intermission and at the conclusion.

"We thought it was silly when we first heard about it," said a Little Rock utility executive. "And it is silly for a small audience. But music works wonders with a larger audience. Try it. You'll be glad you did."

**GET THEM ACQUAINTED WITH EACH OTHER**

You should make it a point to welcome guests and new salesmen. Put them at ease the moment they enter the room. This is common courtesy. Moreover, it helps create the desired atmosphere. Introduce them to others before the meeting is started. Then, when under way, introduce each newcomer to the group. Do it with a big smile, as if it's a pleasure.

Would name badges help in producing a feeling of friendliness? Yes, unless all members of the group are already acquainted with each other. Badges also bolster the individual with a feeling of belonging. Give badges a trial when the circumstances warrant it. But be sure to have the names put in large print so they can be easily read. Unless the names can be read from a distance of two or three feet, the entire effort is wasted.

# HOW TO ENSURE A GOOD AUDIENCE

## HOW TO START YOUR MEETINGS ON TIME

Meetings that start late are as welcome as a blindfold at a burlesque show! It's frustrating, disappointing, and discouraging to be penalized for promptness. That, in effect, is what happens when a meeting is started late. The people who showed on time are penalized for it. Minutes are stolen from their lives because of poor planning.

"Nothing irks me more," said a salesman, "than to sit there until the late-comers have arrived. It takes the *incentive* out of a guy"

Much has been said about starting on time, but little has been said about *how to do it* Here are specific suggestions:

1. Schedule the meeting for an unusual time. Try 9:02 instead of 9:00 or 7:29 instead of 7:30.

Chambers of Commerce throughout the country found that people are more punctual if meetings are not scheduled on the hour or half hour. Booking the get-together at an odd time helps point up the exact minute. It makes you, as well as others, more time conscious. However, having made a point of it, be certain to start on time.

2. Appoint an extroverted sergeant-at-arms. Station him at the door to collect a 25 cent fine from all late-comers at future sessions. Accept no alibis. Make no exceptions—not even top brass! Ultimately, let the group vote on how to use the money collected.

"This has worked better for me than anything else!' said a Grand Rapids executive. "When you're late you get a little kidding along with the fine!"

3. Be sure you have a full agenda. Better to have too much than too little. The fellow who's afraid he will run out of "gas" is inclined to start the meeting late. He's afraid the program will be completed well ahead of schedule, and that this will make him look bad. So he stalls for time. When he finally does begin, he makes things worse by proceeding slowly. The thought of an early finish makes him afraid to plunge into his agenda.

Don't be afraid you'll overload the agenda. Just use some

judgment in which items to omit if you find that you actually have overloaded it.

4. Avoid alibis. "They don't expect me to start on time. Besides they want to visit with each other first." Ever hear excuses like these? If people don't expect a meeting to begin at the proper time it's because prior meetings did not. Poor procedure in the past is no reason for such procedure in the future. As for visiting, anyone desiring to visit simply can do so before the appointed hour instead of after it. Moreover, if visiting is really important it should be included in the agenda. A salesman confided, "Surely—we visit while waiting for the meetings to start. But it's not out of choice. It's because we have nothing else to do. We'd much prefer to skip the visiting and get going with the business at hand."

5. Complete all plans and arrangements well before meeting time. Do everything there is to do. See everyone there is to see.

Many meetings have been started late because the person in charge figures, "I'll see Mac just before the meeting. There'll be plenty of time to work out the details then." Mac may be late. Even if he's on time, there's confusion. Others are arriving. Their greetings and questions make final arrangements difficult. Complete everything ahead of time. You'll be glad you did . . . and so will your audience.

6. Place an alarm clock on the speakers' stand. Set the alarm for the time the session should begin. Watch it closely. If the alarm does not sound off at the proper moment, then cause it to ring anyway. Let it ring for several seconds while the salesmen settle down. After shutting it off, start the program immediately.

"We tried the alarm clock at our meetings," said a Richmond sales supervisor. "It worked so well that we now wonder how we ever did without it. Once your audience expects it, they'll be disappointed if you stop using it."

### HOW TO CREATE INFORMALITY

Meetings should be informal. A feeling of friendship should be established. Because his previous meetings had been too stiff, a Pennsylvania sales manager decided to "let his hair down." He

# HOW *TO* ENSURE A *GOOD* AUDIENCE 119

started his next meeting by terming it a shirt-sleeve session. His first act was to remove his coat and roll up his sleeves. This broke the ice, proving the boss was human after all. A few of the salesmen followed his example, and removed their coats. That meeting proved to be the most beneficial of an entire series, chiefly because good "climate" was established. The salesmen knew from the outset that they could relax and enjoy things. They were more inclined to participate, too.

Here's another way that an informal atmosphere was created: A division manager of an oil company approached the speakers' stand and fired several blank cartridges from a pistol. The moment the last was fired someone yelled, "Hey—what are you doing?" The manager replied, "You said we should start this meeting with a bang, so we just did! Now for our program . . ."

### HOW TO MAKE MONEY TALK

The problem with some audiences is too much informality-even a little "horse play." In such cases you could precondition the audience. Estimate total payroll costs for the time the meeting will consume. Then add any travel or other expenses. The total will be impressive. To dramatize how much the meeting is costing, show the cash equivalent of the cost. Show it in silver dollars. Dump the silver on a table at the front of the room! Then tell them what it represents.

If people attending the meeting are paid on a commission basis, money can be made to speak even louder. First, evaluate the meeting to be conducted. How much can it be worth to each person who applies what he learns? How much could it increase his commission in, say, the next year?

Kick things off by displaying the corresponding amount in silver dollars. You may need a wheel barrow. This will get attention and interest—but good! It will establish a very favorable atmosphere.

"We tried this in Chicago last year," said a shoe manufacturer. "We figured that the meeting could be worth an extra $2,700 to each man who used the material presented.

# 120  HOW *TO ENSURE A GOOD AUDIENCE*

"Did you ever try to get 2,700 silver dollars? We had to go to nine banks! And it took four people to carry it onto the stage. But the idea worked well for us. The men are still talking about it."

### HOW TO MAKE THEM WANT TO LISTEN

Your objective can be better accomplished if the audience knows what you're trying to do. Let your plans be known. If you're simply to give a ten-minute pep talk, tell them that at the outset. If it's an all-day meeting to improve selling practices, then say so.

Give a brief preview. Suggest that they watch for certain highlights to take place. By so doing, you make the audience feel that it's being taken into your confidence. You remove psychological barriers, and establish a common ground. The result is a warmer atmosphere, as well as greater co-operation from the audience.

Above all, point out the benefits to be received. Give them due incentive. Make them want to be a part of what is to follow.

### HOW TO STAY ON SCHEDULE

Starting on time is a *must*. Yet it's no more important than ending on time. By ending on schedule you show consideration for all members of the audience which goes a long way toward creating a good atmosphere at future meetings.

*Hoping* the agenda will be completed at the proper time is not enough. You must work at it. You'll happen to end on time when you cause the happening. Further, an apology for a tardy close won't get you "off the hook."

Allow a specified number of minutes for everything that will take place. Advise each participant that success of the meeting is dependent on his willingness to stay within the allotted time. Then set time aside for emceeing.

How about comments from the audience? Will they be time consuming? If you have any, they *will* be. So allow time for any discussion that might take place. Your schedule will be badly shattered if you do not.

# HOW TO ENSURE A GOOD AUDIENCE

## HOW TO USE A TIMING DEVICE

It seems picayunish to consider a timing device. However, for any meeting of an hour's duration or longer you should use one.

Too many participants get carried away with themselves. Sometimes it's a member of the audience who seems determined to bog things down with unscheduled discussion. A timer takes care of these situations in an impersonal inoffensive way.

"A timing system is as essential as a master of ceremonies/' vowed a man in Houston. "Use any system you like, as long as you do use one. I know—it improved our meetings considerably."

There are several methods of "blowing the whistle" on participants.

An electric device can be obtained from companies that rent public address systems. It consists of three small lights—white for all clear, orange for a two minute warning, and red for overtime. This gadget is attached to the rostrum, where it can be seen only by the speaker. It's a most effective tool for upholding your schedule.

"We use one like this," reported a Baltimore sales manager. "But ours has a buzzer on it. When the red light comes on it starts buzzing. Thereafter, the speaker finds it almost impossible to continue because of the buzzing noise."

When booking a meeting room at a hotel you often find such a gadget available. Hotels tired of overtime meetings long ago. Thus, many hotels provide a timer as part of the p.a. system.

A less ingenious method involves a simple noisemaker, operated by someone seated in the first row. A cricket chirper is often used, although any squeaky toy will do. While amateurish, a noisemaker is none the less effective.

In the absence of a better system, the person responsible for timing stands in the rear of the room. When overtime, he waves his arms like a mad man. It usually works, too. Before long he's bound to be noticed! "I've done this a couple of times," said a hardware executive. "You feel like a fool when you do it, but you certainly keep the meeting on schedule." The smaller the meeting, the more effective you'll find this to be. The greatest objection to it, however, is that most of us get "cold feet" at the last minute. It is somewhat extreme! So the timekeeper is reluctant to go through with it and waits until the proceedings are several minutes behind schedule. Then it's too late, and his wildest arm-waving cannot turn back the clock. The point is this: hand signals will work if they are used with the same precision as other timing devices.

You can interrupt by stating something like: "So that we won't get behind schedule, Joe, will you try to finish in the next couple of minutes?" This is distracting to the audience, but it's better than letting Joe throw you twenty minutes late.

Use judgment, however. If Joe appears to be in the final steps, wait a minute or two. He should close on a high note—not on an interruption by the timekeeper. Risk a minute or so if he seems about to conclude. Then if he doesn't shut up, you can shut him up!

#### THE VALUE OF USING A TIMEKEEPER

Which timing system you choose, is not important. What's important is that you do select one. By adhering to your schedule you're maintaining a good "climate."

But will you personally be able to do the timekeeping? When conducting a sales meeting you have six dozen things to handle. Delegate most of them, including the timekeeping. You shouldn't have to worry about mechanical chores.

"If I had to keep time while doing everything else I'd go crazy," said a fellow in Davenport. "I always get a helper or two from the audience. Why not? Any of our salesmen are glad to help."

While someone else watches the clock, you can watch "the big picture." See that all goes well. Make sure none of the events are misleading. Keep your eyes on the objective of the meeting.

### HOW TO ENSURE A GOOD AUDIENCE

**Put It on a Positive Plane**

**Use the Magic of Music**

**Get Them Acquainted With Each Other**

# HOW *TO ENSURE A GOOD AUDIENCE*

**Start on Time**

**Create Informality**

**Make Them Want to Listen**

**Stay on Schedule**

**Use a Timer**

# 12

# How to Emcee a Sales Meeting

Many people think a master of ceremonies should have a big smile, should say that everything is wonderful, and should tell a joke or two. He should!

The emcee is the spark of the meeting. His smile makes the spark greater. His positive and cheerful attitude causes better reception of the program. And his humor gives a change of pace.

### 16 Ways to Be a Good Emcee

1. Be rehearsed. You can easily "dry run" the emceeing. If necessary, this can be done without the presence of speakers and other participants. For instance, the introduction of speakers can be rehearsed without the help of anyone else. When possible, though, ask one or two people to assist. They can detect possible pitfalls and help you avoid them. The executive who fails to re hearse his emceeing is kidding himself. He will invariably do a better job if he has practiced. Adequate rehearsal results in confidence, improvement, poise and a smoother performance.

2. Anticipate pitfalls. Are some of the subjects likely to cause trouble unless handled skillfully? Should you talk things over with one or two of your speakers?

How about your own material? Anything objectionable in it? Could it possibly cause a stir? How about the other participants?

For example, is there a possibility the boss will mention the

# HOW *TO* EMCEE A SALES MEETING 125

new compensation plan even though the salesmen have not heard about it yet? Will someone ineptly mention a Christmas bonus when the men are sore because no bonus was declared last Christmas?

Perhaps some of the salesmen "broke their picks" on a product that was not salable and which, therefore, has since been discontinued. If so, why let it be mentioned? It's negative. Bury it!

Anticipate things that could happen. Then make sure they don't.

3. Be alive, vibrant. Show some "bounce." It was a sales consultant who told a novice emcee, "If you can't be anything else, be enthusiastic!" This is excellent advice. An unenthusiastic emcee can turn a good meeting into a mediocre meeting or a mediocre meeting into a poor one.

For instance, a sales meeting of furniture dealers was held together by an emcee who "kept the joint jumping." He made every event seem as if it would be the answer to a furniture dealer's problems. The audience could hardly wait for the next speaker or demonstration. The emcee's enthusiasm and bounce made a genuine success of what could have been a weak meeting.

4. Refrain from apologizing.

"We're getting started a little late, but . . ."
"We really intended to . . ."
"We had hoped . . ."
"It's too bad that Mr. Jones could not be with us, but . . ."
"If we had time to do so . . ."
"Had we known about it, we could have . . ."

An apology weakens the meeting. It's an admission that the meeting could be better. So why apologize. It accomplishes nothing good.

5. Introduce speakers properly. Few emcees take the trouble to do this. Invariably a good introduction answers three questions—"What's it about? Why should I listen? Who says so?"

Write the introduction in advance. Put down every word of it. Then practice giving it until you've virtually memorized it. You weaken the introduction if you are obviously reading it.

## SAMPLE INTRODUCTION

"What's it about?"   The next talk is on objections. There'll be demonstrations on how to overcome all the common objections—price, not interested—all of them.

"Why should I listen?"   This information will help you with every prospect. You can use it to close more sales and make more money.

"Who says so?"   One of the best salesmen on the staff will handle this subject. He's the man who won last year's Distinguished Sales Award—a real go-getter—Jim McBride!

For formal occasions, an introduction can be more lengthy. But 30 seconds should be a maximum. Let the speaker do the speech making.

"We present Jim McBride!" sounds better than "I give you Jim McBride!"

Another tip—save the speaker's name until last. Then when stating his name, really bear down! Example: "Hailing from Davenport, Iowa, here's FRED BUSHER!"

It's usually a good idea to check with the speaker beforehand to get his approval of the introduction. A misstatement in the introduction may upset the speaker, get him off to a bad start.

6. Wait for *the* speaker *to get there.* If you leave the rostrum before his arrival, you create a void, a lull. Attention is lost when there's no one to hold attention. You should wait for him at the speakers' stand.

Shake the speaker's hand when he arrives at the stand. Give him a verbal pat on the back with something like: "Let 'em have it, Joe!" He may need your encouragement.

The manager of an accounting department once said, "I make few speeches. So, naturally, I was scared to death! But when I reached the platform the emcee was waiting for me. He shook hands firmly and said, 'Give 'em 'ell, Ed. You're just the one to do it!' This gave me the confidence I really needed at that time."

7. *Assist the speaker.* There may be several things you can do for him: adjust the height of the mike, hold a visual, or distribute

# HOW TO EMCEE A SALES MEETING

take-home sheets. Don't feel that the speaker is working for you. While he's on the platform, you're working for him. Your assistance will improve his presentation. This upgrades your meeting. A Salt Lake City manufacturer reported, "When I'm asked to emcee an important meeting, I use the 'buddy system.' That is, I assign someone to assist each speaker. The 'buddy' contacts the speaker beforehand and offers to help in any way he can. It makes the speaker's job easier—the emcee's too."

8. *Show* your own interest. From time to time the audience will note what you're doing. If you obviously appreciate each event, the audience will be more appreciative. Refrain from wandering around the room and whispering to others. Get "lost" in the program.

9. Don't remake a speech. Nothing is more boring than a speech about a speech. The speaker presumably researched his subject and made a planned presentation. How could you hope to "top" him with "off the cuff" remarks? A rehash is anticlimactical. Don't bore the audience with your version of each subject. It won't be appreciated. "Post-mortems are for the doctors," said a Providence, Rhode Island, executive. "At sales meetings, they're for the birds!"

When thanking a speaker, you might refer to one or two points in a favorable way. But be brief about it. Then move on to the next event.

10. *Use* humor. When the participants pull lots of gags, you can "soft-pedal" your own jokes. But usually there's not enough humor unless the emcee injects some. The best humor is related to your subject matter. Unrelated humor is nothing but entertainment. But don't joke about the subject coming up. It puts the next speaker at a disadvantage. He will have difficulty getting attention. His approach to the subject will at first seem anticlimactical. Instead, you should joke about the subject just completed.

Resist the urge to tell an off-color story. If there's a possibility that someone will be offended, the risk is too great. Don't take it. There's no need to "take a chance" when acceptable humor is abundant.

Good joke books can be purchased in any book store. Further, radio and TV comedians hand out a wealth of usable material every day.

Stories about minority groups are dangerous, especially if the minority group or one of its members is the butt of the story. Forego all stories involving color, race, or creed. Not only are such stories in poor taste but many people consider them to be un-American.

Tell jokes on yourself. People will then laugh louder! But don't tell jokes on the audience. Such humor falls flat.

The wise emcee never depreciates a story by beginning it with: "You may have heard this one before, but . . ." If you're going to tell it, tell it. Why make it sound like a repeat job that's hardly worth hearing?

11. Make everyone feel important. The audience, or any individual in it, will be more receptive if made to feel important. Those for whom you have a liking and respect will usually respect you. Above all, don't belittle. The emcee who "talks down" to his audience is unpopular. So are his meetings.

> Wrong way: "You said you wanted help on pricing. I don't see why it should be a problem to you. There's nothing difficult about it. But since some of you apparently have still not learned the pricing procedure, I'll make another attempt to explain it to you."
>
> *Right way:* "You said you wanted help on pricing. We think you guys are pretty terrific. So if that's what you want, that's what you'll get. Watch closely, because here we go!"

12. *Get,* and keep, participation. Who's more interested in a football game—the players or the spectators? The players are more interested. They never take their eyes off the ball. Spectators, to the contrary, fumble with cigarettes, hot dogs and thermos bottles. Try to get everybody into the act so they'll be "players." They'll be much more interested. Have the men switch coats or ties, change seats, don funny hats, count off, sing or recite. They'll love it!

# HOW *TO* EMCEE A SALES MEETING

13. Make *light* of disturbances. Don't fight them. When you lose your composure, you lose "face."

If a fire truck zips by with siren open, pause for the noise to die down. Then smile while quipping: "I told you this new sales plan was hot!" If a second one drowns you out a moment later: "It's not only hot, but red hot!"

Late arrivals sometimes are disturbing. But don't call them down with bitter words. If something must be said: "There are some more chairs over here, gentlemen."

Two people in the audience often will talk to each other. There are various ways of handling this. For example, a school teacher says, "What you're talking about must be quite interesting for you to interrupt and disturb. Why don't you tell us about it?" Or the blasé" night club emcee tells a loudmouth, "Hey you—the one doing the talking. Let's play horsy. I'll be the head and shoulders. You just be your natural self!"

But a sales executive cannot embarrass members of his audience—not even those who deserve it. Morale must be upheld. Besides, other salesmen may sympathize with the offenders. Be more subtle. Start talking very loudly or beat the lectern while continuing with the business at hand.

14. Keep *it* under control. Either you are in charge or the audience is. Be courteous, but don't permit chaos.

"It's a weak emcee who lets things get out of hand." These words came from the manufacturer of a brand of clothing well-known to all. "My last sales manager did everything else fairly well, but he could not control a sales meeting. I finally had to let him go. There was no alternative. Sales *meetings* are important and complete *control is* a must."

If things get out of hand, call for order. Take a tip from the judge who bangs the bench with a gavel. Rap the speakers' stand three or four times with your fist. Or have a police whistle handy. It restores order in a hurry!

15. Make *it move*. No other rule is more important than this one. The meeting that drags between events is a poor meeting.

Speak fast, act fast, be fast! In this case, haste does not make waste. Remember—you can overdo a number of things—from

A to Z—but one of the things "hardest" to overdo, is enthusiasm/ When permitted to do so, your audience will often bog things down with discussion. Don't permit it. Tell them, "I wish we had time for a comment from everyone, but . . ." or "If anyone wants to discuss this further, I'll gladly meet with you after we have adjourned. But, right now . . ."

16. *Give credits before the climax.* Thank everyone there is to thank. But don't wait until the last minute to do it. It was a member of the Toastmasters' Club who said, "When you've finally put them on Cloud 19, leave them there!"

As developed more fully in the next chapter, acknowledgments at the end of a meeting take some of the fire out of it. Thank speakers and others before the final event.

### HOW TO EMCEE A SALES MEETING

Be Rehearsed

Anticipate Pitfalls

Introduce Speakers Properly

Be Alive, Vibrant

Refrain From Apologizing

Wait for Speakers to Get There

Assist the Speakers

Show Your Own Interest

Don't Remake a Speech

Use Humor

Make Everyone Feel Important

Get And Keep Participation

Make Light of Disturbances

Keep It Under Control

Make It Move Give Credits

Before the Climax

# 13

# How to Climax Your Sales Meeting

Think back to the most exciting football game it's been your pleasure to see. Wasn't there some last minute scoring? Something happened to cause a supreme peak of interest at the end. A dazzling broken field run, a dramatic goal line stand, or something climactic served as the frosting on the cake. A rousing conclusion makes an average event good, and a good event better.

What happens at the end of a "horse opera"? The villain gets his just deserts and the hero kisses the girl—or the horse! Thus the play is climaxed. All of the scenes preceding were nothing but build-up to the triumphant conclusion. As the drama ends, the audience is left with a feeling of completeness and satisfaction.

A grand finale is often used to climax a musicale. A mystery, on the other hand, may end with a surprise twist which reveals the suspicious looking butler was innocent after all. But what about sales meetings? Shouldn't they be climaxed?

**EVERY SALES MEETING SHOULD BE CLIMAXED**

Yes, every sales meeting should be planned toward a climax. There should be a supreme peak of interest at the end of the agenda. Only one such highlight should be planned. Two features would detract from each other. All the events preceding it should serve as build-up which sets the stage for the climax. As the various events are staged, the pitch should become faster and faster until the close. By planning your meetings in this way you'll get much more interest in them. A good ending leaves the salesmen with a sweet taste in their mouths. It makes them willing to come back for more.

**FACTS ABOUT SEMICLIMAXES**

Sales meetings are often so long that recesses are necessary. It's a good idea to reach a semi climax just before every break. This prompts favorable comment during the intermission. It leaves everyone wanting more. It gives the impression that your meeting is being moved into high gear, that the next session consequently will be even more interesting.

You should also strike a high note immediately after intermission. This solves the problem of quieting the audience. "Get it going again with a bang!" This is the advice of a textiles man. "We hit a semiclimax after every intermission. In this way we recapture the attention of the audience." There's another advantage, though. A good start creates the feeling that events to follow are worthy of full attention. The result is a better audience.

**HOW TO GUARD AGAINST AN ANTICLIMAX**

This is a book of "do's"-not a book of "don't's." Yet a few "don't's" will work wonders toward preventing an anticlimax.

DON'T let a semi climax outshine the conclusion of your meeting. The major highlight should invariably be last.

DON'T summarize after the climax. Do it earlier. While summation helps get your message across, it's not sufficiently colorful to serve as the climax.

DON'T thank participants at the end of the meeting. Anytime before will do. An expression of thanks at the end takes the edge off things.

DON'T stall around if you finish early. Conclude the meeting ahead of time. A stall is anticlimactic.

DON'T leave the impression you're closing the meeting merely because you've run out of topics: "Well, if there's nothing else to cover . . ."

DON'T acknowledge a raised hand when you're bringing the

# HOW TO CLIMAX YOUR SALES MEETING 133

meeting to a close. Ignore it. See the individual later. His question or comment would have taken the frosting off the cake.

DON'T let a comment from the floor cause a long discussion at the last minute. If someone speaks up even though not invited to do so, make him be brief. Brush him off politely but quickly.

DON'T let someone in the audience have the last word, or even the nexWo-last. There's no reason to believe he will say something to help you close on a high note. Regain control of the situation. Then close it yourself.

DON'T ignore the obvious. It usually is evident that the audience will want to know some fact, such as the time of the next session or date of the next meeting. Anticipate these things. Supply the information so there won't be anticlimactic last minute questions from the floor.

DON'T be indefinite or indecisive. Conclude with vigor. An aggressive plumbing executive in Knoxville often closes with "Let's go get 'em!"

DON'T thank the audience for attending, especially near the close. If you've conducted a sparkling meeting, the audience should thank you!

### 14 Ways to Climax a Sales Meeting

1. An effective method of ending on a high note is to announce a new policy or procedure. This works only when the change will be welcomed by the group. An unexpected holiday, a Christmas bonus, increased travel allowances—any of these would go over with a bang! But the change need not involve a gratuity. It could be the elimination of an unpopular, detailed daily report. Or the announcement of a system for handling suggestions of the sales men, suggestions that previously were ignored.

"I'll never forget the meeting we held last summer," said a Vermont business owner. "Things had been going pretty well. And we climaxed it by announcing that the men could approve their own mileage reports. This meant they'd get their expense money sooner, of course. Did they like it? They went wild!"

2. A new sales aid can serve as a climax.

## 134 HOW TO CLIMAX YOUR SALES MEETING

For example, if new sample cases are to be distributed, make a production of it! Let introduction of the cases climax a sales meeting. That way the new cases will mean more than if merely "handed out with the rations." But, more related to our purpose here, the meeting will be better received because of its climactic ending.

A company dealing in waterproofing franchises perfected a standard sales presentation. The announcement of this long awaited sales tool was followed by the distribution of printed copies. It made a rousing climax.

3. Merchandising literature is constantly produced by manufacturers and marketing firms. A new piece of literature can be used to bring a meeting to a very effective close.

DON'T read the new material aloud. That would be boring. Shout about it! Sing its praises! Tell what it will do for all who use it properly.

A department store buyer said, "I finally realized that we could get manufacturers' leaflets on most of our items. These leaflets help in several ways, especially in ending a meeting on a high note."

4. A new ad or advertising campaign can top things off in a large way. Consult the persons who produced the advertising. Learn more about it. Then spring it at the close, making a huge "to do" over it.

An office machine company official said, "The announcement of our new advertising is an ideal way to climax a sales meeting. We get much good out of the motivation it gives our salesmen. That motivation is almost as valuable as the new customers pulled by the ad."

5. An addition to the product line *is* a fitting climax.

Let's assume there's a need for the new item, or else it would not be added to the line. For maximum build-up, earlier events should point up the need. If nothing else, use remarks such as, "It would be wonderful if we had an item that would fit that particular need, but of course, we don't." A comment or two of this sort adds much to the big moment.

# HOW *TO CLIMAX* YOUR SALES MEETING

6. Next year's line—new models—serve the purpose well.

A costume jewelry official in New York declared, "Our new lines are always shown at sales meetings. It's the best introduction the merchandise can get. We climax the meeting with it. Then everyone examines the new line."

In the case of clothing, garments for the next season are appropriate. Regardless of the nature of the merchandise, however, usher it in with fanfare. Unveil it in a way that surprises the audience. Display it in the most attractive manner possible.

7. The enthusiastic announcement of a sales contest will do the trick. Make a big thing of it. Don't take an hour to do it, giving all the details. Instead, hit only the high spots. Emphasize what can be won by those who really go, Go, GO! This is not only good for the sales meeting, it's also good for the contest.

8. When a contest has recently ended, avoid the natural desire to name winners at the beginning of your next sales meeting. It's better to recognize winners during the last few minutes.

By holding the audience in suspense, a greater climax is generated. You could even do a little teasing as the meeting progresses: "I surely wish we could tell you who won the prizes, but it will be sometime before the winners are named." This is like throwing gasoline on a fire!

9. The presentation of achievement awards can be made to fill the bill. For instance, length-of-service pins are often presented as the feature attraction. Certificates of completion of sales training courses have also been awarded.

"We have a few people to be honored at every meeting," stated a hotel manager. "The recognition is good for morale. Besides, it helps bring the meeting to a satisfactory conclusion."

10. A fast inspirational speech can produce the desired effect. But be careful—a real spellbinder is needed. Get someone dynamic. This type of climax is more effective when used with a large crowd. A speaker can inspire a few hundred people more easily than a handful.

The person to deliver this Sunday punch should be kept in the background until time for him to speak. There's nothing climactic

**136    HOW *TO CLIMAX YOUR SALES MEETING***

about hearing from the same person a second or third time. Also, a wind-up speech should be brief and should not carry the burden of training. It's for inspiration.

11. Many suitable gimmicks can be devised—souvenirs, novelty give-aways.

An eastern life insurance company used a fake newspaper. Bold headlines called attention to a new insurance policy being introduced. The copy was dummy stuff—dateless background material used over and over with different headlines. During the meeting there was subtle mention of need for that type of policy. There finally came a hint that the policy some day might be produced. Then, just before the meeting ended, a newsboy appeared on the scene. He screamed at the top of his voice, showing everyone the bogus headline—"Sensational New Policy Electrifies Insurance Industry!"

After the emcee confirmed the birth of the new policy, he closed the session. Each salesman was given one of the newspapers as he left the room.

12. Still another method of climaxing is the surprise entry of wives and sweethearts. Arrange for them to appear unexpectedly, followed by a social event of some sort. This works best at certain meetings, such as those near Christmas or Valentine's Day.

Where the agenda is based on long range goals, however, most men give thought to their families. Major goals involve new homes and the like. So that's another time when wives and sweethearts can appropriately cap the proceedings.

"We had the wives and sweethearts appear unexpectedly at a regional meeting last fall," reported the division manager of a large oil company. "It was quite effective, well worth the effort and expense."

13. Meditation has successfully been used at large sales meetings. Ask everyone to stand, to lower his head, and to think. "Let's meditate for a moment . . . Just think . . . Think of this meeting and what we've accomplished. Think of how you can use this wealth of information. Think."

Drop your voice, both in volume and tone. Then continue more slowly with "Think of the wonderful opportunity we have." Pause.

# HOW *TO CLIMAX* YOUR SALES MEETING

"Think of the many customers we're serving, the big job that's being done." Pause, lowering your voice still more. "Think of the many additional people we should be serving." Pause. "Let's resolve to get and to serve these many additional customers." Pause longer. "Let's serve more people, while also helping ourselves. We can do it, we *will* do it. Good luck and good night."

This type of climax won't send them home shouting. But if preceded by a good meeting it can be quite dramatic and effective. It will send them home inspired to do a bigger job than ever.

14. The surprise appearance of a V.I.P. is another twist. A very high company official, for instance, can effectively be presented in this manner. Just be sure he's so important the men deem it a privilege to "rub elbows" with him.

The unexpected presentation of a prominent public office holder can also produce a glossy finish for you.

Whether it's the big boss or a big politician, don't let him make a long-winded speech. You want a *climax]*

### HOW TO CLIMAX YOUR SALES MEETINGS

Announce a Welcomed Policy or Procedure

Distribute a New Sales Aid

Tell of New Merchandising Literature

Spring a New Ad or Advertising Campaign

Play Up an Addition to Your Product Line

Show Next Year's Models

Announce a Contest

Name Contest Winners

Present Achievement Awards

Use a Fast Inspirational Speech

Devise a Gimmick Enter Wives

and Sweethearts

Use Meditation Surprise

Them With a V.I.P.

# 14. How to Conduct Group Training Sessions

Introduction is one thing. Training is another. Telling people to do things is not training. You can repeatedly tell workers what to do. You can also tell them how to do it. But when all is said and done, more has been said than done! The workers cannot perform the task. Why? Because they have not been trained.

Training is more than talking. It includes demonstration. Show how to do the thing being taught. Then comes the big step. Have *the* learners try out. Let them demonstrate their knowledge. Get them to practice and drill. Training is the development of proper habits. When a salesman is trained, he reacts automatically to any situation. He does the right thing by habit—without delay or confusion.

### How to Teach Groups Effectively

**I. PREPARE YOURSELF**

A butane gas company switched to a new system of credit and collections. The owner of the company called a meeting to announce the change. When asked how he'd present the new plan, the owner replied, 'Til tell them about it. What did you expect me to do? Draw a picture?"

As it turned out, he actually should have drawn a picture. Maybe two! Few people understood him. Several salesmen made mistakes in the days following, and some were costly.

The point is significant. *The* instructor *should* prepare. A

# HOW TO CONDUCT GROUP TRAINING SESSIONS   139

knowledge of the subject is a must. But the method of presenting that knowledge should also be prepared. Spend twice as much time in preparation as you do in teaching. For a 30-minute training session, devote at least an hour to preparation. More if needed. Preparation results in quicker learning. It saves man hours and payroll costs. This is reason enough to prepare thoroughly.

### II. PREPARE YOUR AUDIENCE

Before presenting your topic, prepare your audience for it.

First, put the audience at ease. Tell a joke or two. Do whatever is necessary to create a pleasant learning situation.

Then eliminate anything that's bothering the audience. Do some people have questions? If so, give answers. Clear the air. Remove everything that might act as a mental block.

Explain what you're going to teach. Be specific. Example—"Men, we're going to learn about the new order book. You'll learn exactly how to use it." This ties it down. The audience knows what to expect. Moreover, the audience knows what you expect.

Make it interesting. Romance it. Give the background, the history, the why, the wherefore. "We thought our order form was perfect. It was perfect at the time it was adopted. But times have changed. It no longer gives you the information you need.

"For example, there's no room on the form for shipping instructions. Consequently, a separate note must be attached to every order. That means time and trouble on your part.

"Also, the blank spaces are too small. There's not enough room to describe the article being purchased. Skimpy descriptions have resulted in misunderstandings and occasionally the wrong item has been shipped."

Explain why the audience should be receptive. "By using the new order form, you'll save time and trouble. Your customers will get better service. Thus, you'll make more money."

Make them want to learn.

### III. PRESENT YOUR MATERIAL

A convoy of ships is geared to the speed of the slowest ship. Likewise, teaching is geared to the speed of the slowest learner. Present the information slowly and clearly. Offer it in proper sequence—first things first. Take only one step at a time. Present no more than the learner can master. Give it in "bite-size" portions. While he can eat 21 meals this week, he can digest only a little at a time. Likewise, he can learn only a little at a time.

Both tell and show. If you need help in showing it, arrange for assistance. Dramatize it.

Keep it positive. Teaching what to do is enough to learn. Don't burden them with what *not* to do. If you've taught the right things and they're doing them, they cannot possibly be doing the wrong things.

Suppose you were in the audience. Imagine yourself as the newest salesman. How would it sound to you? How would it look? Would you understand it? Would you start using the new information?

### IV. HAVE THEM LEARN BY DOING

Have the group practice. Let them apply the information during your meeting.

"Three articles of merchandise are listed on the blackboard. Let's assume you sold those articles. The name of your customer is shown at the bottom of the blackboard. There's his address, the date, and details of shipping. Now fill out an order form based on this information."

Role playing is often used. For instance, suppose you're teaching how to overcome objections. You play the part of a customer, while a member of the audience acts as the salesman. Keep it serious. "Ham it up" too much and you ruin it. After a couple of demonstrations, have the men pair off. Let them practice and drill on each other. This is real training!

Correct mistakes. Reteach where necessary. To facilitate this step, learning by doing, training sessions should be small. Large crowds are difficult to handle. The people get in each other's way. A rule of thumb suggests that training meetings be limited to 30 people.

### CHECK ON LEARNING

Hold yourself responsible. Whether your salesmen are smart enough to learn is not open to question. The question is whether

# HOW *TO CONDUCT GROUP TRAINING SESSIONS* 141

you're smart enough to teach! If they haven't learned, it's because you haven't taught.

Check their understanding. There are two ways to check. First, ask questions. "What should be done next? Why? Is that the best way of doing it? How do we know?"

A second means of checking is by observing performance. Can they perform the task in the meeting? Has every person demonstrated his ability to perform?

Once they've mastered it in the classroom, have them apply the lesson in the field. The sooner they apply it, the better they will remember it. Besides, practical application *is the* ultimate *objective ofi all* group training.

### Appeal to as Many Senses as Possible

There are five senses—sight, touch, smell, taste, and hearing. We learn through all five. You should appeal to as many senses as possible. Let the group learn all they're willing to learn through the sense of hearing. Then go to work on the other four. Let 'em see it, touch it, smell it, and taste it. Many subjects cannot be directed toward all of the five senses. But *every* subject can be aimed toward two or more of the senses. Most things can be beamed toward at least three senses.

How could your audience hear the durability of wallpaper? Pull the ends apart suddenly. It will pop the paper like a shine-boy cracking a shoe rag! The audience actually hears the strength of the paper.

How can your audience be convinced that shoes are well made? Pass them around. Let everyone take a sniff. Good leather smells like good leather!

### How to Sugarcoat Your Training

Salesmen want training. Why not? It saves time for them, makes their work easier, increases their earning power, and prepares them for bigger jobs.

They want training. But they don't want it called "training." There's something about the word that depreciates the people being taught. It makes them feel subordinated. Thus many companies hold sales meetings instead of training meetings. They offer executive development programs—not courses. They conduct *sessions* rather than classes.

A company engaged in direct to consumer sales has discontinued training meetings. Instead, *information* meetings are conducted. Their salespeople don't like the thought of being trained. They do want information, however. Result: attendance, which is voluntary, is up 17 percent.

Each presentation should be interesting. Inject humor and animation. Merchandise your training. Sell it. Training can be enjoyable. Make it that way!

### 10 Ways to Make Sales Training More Interesting

1. The steps in a sale are attention, interest, desire, and action. A Distributive Education instructor in Texas presents this information in an interesting way. He likens the steps to the courses in a meal.

"A colorful fruit cocktail gets your *attention* the moment you're seated for dinner. A salad follows. This gets your interest in a big way. It really whets your appetite. Then comes the entree. You look at it and gleefully inhale the aroma. Your desire is at its peak! After the entree, you take final action by eating dessert."

Pictures of the four courses were pasted on flocking material and used with a slap board. It made a very effective presentation. The steps in a sale were more easily learned because they were related to something the learners already knew.

2. A furniture store owner made a list of questions most frequently asked by prospective customers. He put each question on a separate 3" x 5" index card.

In a training session, he shuffled the cards and dealt them to his salespeople. "They got a big kick out of trying to answer the questions," he reported. "Also, a lecture would not have caused half as much learning."

3. Enthusiasm has been dramatized in many ways. When teaching people to "bubble over," you can make it interesting by drop-

# HOW *TO CONDUCT GROUP TRAINING SESSIONS*

ping a couple of bromos in a full glass of water. Your audience will remember it. So will the janitor!

This may not prompt enthusiasm before the prospect, however. So give each man a card.

> The presentation I'm about to make is backed by a twenty-million-dollar organization. Our product line is the finest in the world! When I see my next prospect, I'll be red hot—sizzling! Do I have enthusiasm? Watch my smoke!!!

Ask your men to read this card before *each call.* While enthusiasm is intangible, it can be taught.

4. A professional sales trainer in Minnesota has a unique method of teaching persistence. He used a jack-in-the-box.

"Your prospect doesn't buy. So what?" The trainer released the jack and said, "You call on him again."

"He still doesn't buy." Again he released the jack, stating, "So you turn up at his office again."

"He turns you down another time." The jack is released. "But you pop up again."

"One of you finally gives up." The jack is released. "Let it be the prospect—not you!"

Application of the teaching point is difficult in a meeting. However, it can easily be made in the field.

Some firms give a persistence award. It goes to the salesman who makes the greatest number of calls on a single prospect without getting an order. The purpose is not to commend failure, but to commend effort. Without effort there can be no achievement.

5. The motive for buying is a significant part of salesmanship. When a salesman can detect the buying motive, he appeals to it. He magnifies it, elaborates on it. This produces sales—but fast!

An appliance dealer determined that his merchandise was purchased for four reasons: pride of ownership, economy, pleasure, and utility. He uses role playing to teach the recognition of these motives.

The dealer acts as a prospect. He makes statements and asks questions that are clues to buying motives. Example: "Is this like the one you sold Mrs. Astor on Park Row?" The buying motive is pride of ownership—keeping up with the Joneses.

The first salesman to recognize a motive is called upon to explain his opinion. This results in participation, recognition, and *solid training*.

6. The close of a sale begins at the beginning of a sales presentation. While the first step in a sale is to get attention, this step is also the first part of the close.

All steps in a sale must lead toward the close. Unless they do, there will be no close. They so directly lead into the close that they're actually a part of the closing.

An interesting method of presenting this is to hold up a snake. "The close of a sale is like a snake's tail. It begins at the head." If a live snake is to be used, salesmen with weak hearts should not be seated in the front row!

7. Trial closes must be taught. Most companies have standard trial closes, such as. "Does this look like the one you want?" Or, "We can install that for you tomorrow."

Balloons filled with natural gas have been used as "trial balloons." A marketing firm executive released a balloon each time he demonstrated a trial close. "When the prospect appears ready to buy, you send up a trial balloon. For instance, you could ask if the prospect wants his purchase gift wrapped." At this point the executive released a balloon which floated to the ceiling. He continued with additional trial closes, each time lofting a "trial balloon." This made the trial closes stand out. During the application part of the training session, each salesman was given an opportunity to send up "trial balloons."

8. A personnel trainer was teaching the various methods of closing a sale. He made his presentation more effective by using a clothes line, strung across the front of the room. Using clothes pins, he attached placards to the line, each with a word printed on it. One contained the word "ASK," representing always ask for the order. "ALTERNATIVE" covered a choice between something and something, not between something and nothing.

# HOW *TO CONDUCT GROUP TRAINING SESSIONS* 145

"MINOR" stood for closing on a minor issue. In all, there were seven placards as visuals. More was accomplished here:

After the placards were explained, they were distributed to seven of the salesmen. Demonstrations were then conducted. When one of the closing techniques was demonstrated, the salesman holding the pertinent placard pinned it to the clothes line. The cards were frequently redistributed, keeping everyone on his toes.

9. It's difficult to teach salespeople when to stop talking. Some supervisors say, "Get the order and get out." Others say, "Leave within two minutes after the order is signed." But there's usually more to it than that.

The purchase of additional items usually should be suggested. Then too, every sales situation is different. So it's difficult to apply rigid rules. But a general warning is certainly in order. A manufacturer in Virginia begins his warning with a casket. The salesmen are asked to guess the identity of the corpse. "The casket contains the corpse of a sale. It's a sale that was killed by a man who couldn't stop talking!" This bizarre method of getting across the point has been remembered by all who have seen it. Men have commented on it ten years later.

But that isn't all. Transcripts of actual closes are distributed and read. Each is discussed. Questions are asked. "Did the salesman in this script know when to stop talking? If he talked too much, where did the surplus yakking begin? What can each of you do to avoid the same mistake?"

10. People selling over the counter must continuously be trained in suggestion selling. Any clerk can sell what the customer wants. A good salesperson suggests the purchase of additional items.

Here's how a department store buyer demonstrated the power of suggestion . . . She obtained a new perfume atomizer and filled it with colored water. In a training session she gingerly sprayed the room. The spray had absolutely no scent. "That's a delicate scent. What is it? Can anyone say? I'll give you a clue. It's either lilac or rose. Which is it?" The audience of 22 people sniffed for several seconds. Someone voiced his decision. Then others. There was divided opinion. Nine decided on lilac, another

# 146 HOW *TO CONDUCT GROUP TRAINING SESSIONS*

nine on rose. Only four could not smell anything! Having proved that suggestion is powerful, the buyer then conducted an effective training session on suggestion selling.

### How to Use True-False Tests

The true-false quiz is an excellent teaching device. It can make the session more interesting, too. Devise an all inclusive quiz. Every important area, then, is certain to be discussed. Also, the quiz serves as a good review of the highlights. Most people think a quiz is for testing the learners. It is not. It's a test of the instructor. It shows how well he taught.

#### SAMPLE QUIZ ON APPROACHES

Type of Selling: Over the counter.

1. There are three types of approaches.               TRUE    FALSE
2. The salutation approach is always used on friends, TRUE    FALSE
3. "May I help you?" is an overworked service approach.
                                                      TRUE    FALSE
4. "What may I show you?" is a good service approach, TRUE    FALSE
5. A merchandise approach saves time.                 TRUE    FALSE
6. The customer's name should not be used in the approach.
                                                      TRUE    FALSE
7. Tell a waiting customer, "I'll be with you in a moment."
                                                      TRUE    FALSE
8. You should never have anything in your hands during the approach.
                                                      TRUE    FALSE

After the quiz has been distributed and scored, discuss each question.

"Who has the answer to the first one . . . False? You're right—that's false! But what's the main idea there? So what should you do as a result?"

The important thing is to bring out the underlying teaching point. How the individual answered the question is not significant. What the group finally learned about it—that's the thing.

Multiple choice and completion type questions can also be used. True-false is usually best, however, because it's so simple.

Don't grade adults. They resent it. Instead, let each person correct his own paper. They'll usually want a "yardstick," so give it to them: "If you missed only three, you did very well. If you missed less than three, you should be the instructor!"

Let them keep their tests. Encourage a review at some future date. But avoid a school room atmosphere. Adults absolutely will not accept it. They left school long ago and they're not going back!

**HOW TO CONDUCT GROUP TRAINING SESSIONS**

**Prepare Yourself**

**Prepare Your Audience**

**Present Your Material**

**Have Them Learn by Doing**

**Check on Learning**

**Appeal to as Many Senses as Possible**

**Coat It With Sugar**

# 15            How to Publicize Your Sales Meetings

Many sales meetings need little publicity. Some need a great deal. An in-store meeting is easily promoted. Employees are paid to attend and have no choice in the matter. "Captive" groups can be assembled readily. Word-of-mouth is usually sufficient. Then there's the employee bulletin board, the house organ, and the store p.a. system.

But attendance at certain sales meetings is optional. Franchised dealers, for example, can often retain their franchises without attending meetings conducted by the wholesaler or the manufacturer. To get their attendance, there must be real promotion.

Trade associations have the same difficulty. Members must *want* to attend. Sales meetings, therefore, are publicized. Meetings must be sold.

There's often another reason for publicizing a meeting. The product concerned is brought to the attention of the public. This publicity is good public relations. It's gratis advertising.

### Promotional Bulletins and Publicity Releases

There are two reasons why certain sales meetings should be publicized. First, to get attendance. Second, to advertise your product. Now let's discuss *how* to publicize your meetings.

Note the product publicity in this example of a newspaper story. (Such releases are often furnished to papers as discussed on page 150.)

# HOW TO PUBLICIZE YOUR SALES MEETINGS

### APPLIANCE DEALERS CONVENE HERE

Appliance dealers from six states meet here today and tomorrow.

Guests of the Ajax Range Co., they will be shown why it is quicker and safer to cook with gas.

More than 300 dealers are expected. Headquarters are being set up at the Royal Hotel.

Local sponsors are the Smith Furniture & Appliance Store and the Oak Cliff Stop-Shop.

Highlight of the meeting will be introduction of the new Ajax models.

"We have some beautiful new styling," announced Ajax President Richard Roe. Also, there's a model to fit the pocketbook of every family in the country."

Introduction of the new line will climax Wednesday's session. Dealer of the Year will be crowned on Thursday.

## HOW TO PREPARE PROMOTIONAL LEAFLETS

Promotional leaflets can do a good selling job. Put "sock" in them! Make them exciting and appealing. Requirements of an effective mailing piece:

1. It should be attractive. Use art work.
2. It should reflect the theme of the meeting.
3. It should be easily read—no fine print.
4. It should have an interest-getting element.
5. It should tell who, what, when, where.
6. It should emphasize BENEFITS to be gained.
7. It should make registration seem simple.

## HOW TO PREPARE PROMOTIONAL LETTERS

A promotional letter will often "ring the bell." Frame your letter around the four steps in a sale—attention, interest, desire, action.

## 150   HOW TO PUBLICIZE YOUR SALES MEETINGS

        Mr. John Bright Sell
        Rite Store, Inc.
        Anytown, U.S.A.

Attention:   A small fortune in one day! Seems impossible, but is it?

Interest:   Many dealers, like yourself, handle our merchandise. You're doing a terrific job, too. But some of you expressed a desire to do even better. You suggested a sales meeting. You felt that more product information was needed. You also asked for tips on selling this particular line.

Desire:   You can have exactly what you want. We'll give you an all-day meeting chock-full of money making ideas. There'll be exhibits, displays, demonstrations, prizes, and surprises. You'll love it! Your sales will zoom upwards because of this fabulous meeting!

Action:   We'll convene from 9:30 a.m. to 4:30 p.m. on Saturday, June 6th, at the Jefferson Hotel. Please be our guest for lunch that day. And if you care to bring an assistant, that's fine. Two tickets are enclosed.

        No reply is expected. Just be there!

                            Cordially,

                            J. C. MCNAMARA
                            President

Newspaper publicity can easily be obtained provided your releases are of interest to the public. The information must be of general interest.

The meeting itself may be of little concern to the average reader. But there's some phase or feature of the meeting that will make good copy. Slant your story in such a way that everyone will want to read it.

Your sales meeting will not command as much attention in large city newspapers. In New York, Chicago, and Los Angeles, for example, sales meetings are in progress at all times. More than 1,000 conventions per year are held in each of these cities. A meeting there is "just another meeting." In smaller cities, however, your sales meeting can be big news.

# HOW TO PUBLICIZE YOUR SALES MEETINGS

## HOW TO USE THE SIX MAJOR NEWS ANGLES

1. *The meeting itself.* The basic idea that a meeting will be conducted is of some news value. Larger meetings are naturally of greater interest.

Don't tell what the meeting will mean to the minority attending. Explain what it will mean to the *majority* of readers, the many people who will not attend.

Example: "If you're asked to buy a foreign auto, don't be surprised. Foreign Cars, Inc., importers of three European automobiles, will conduct a sales rally tomorrow at the Bluebonnet Hotel. Auto dealers will be shown how to contact more prospective buyers.

"See the People" is the theme of the meeting. Every resident of the area probably will be seen, too. An all-out sales promotion is planned.

"Some 45 dealers are. . . ."

2. *Visiting* fireman. An expert is a guy from out of town. His opinion may receive little attention at home. But if he's a specialist from out of state, he's "copy."

Your principal speaker should have something newsworthy to say, even if you must put the words in his mouth! He can be pictured and quoted on arrival. Or an account of his speech can be featured.

Example: " 'Consumer credit is the backbone of the economy,' declared Jim Starr, credit specialist from Denver, Colorado. 'Credit makes sales and keeps employment high.'

"Starr is here for a meeting of . . ."

Newspapers sometimes request advance copies of the principal speech. When arranging for the principal speaker, let him know if extra copies of his speech may be needed for publicity purposes.

3. Local personality. Readers are always interested in local people.

First, what local people are sponsoring the meeting? Who's making arrangements at the local level? What local people will speak? Will the mayor make a welcoming address? What local companies or agencies are involved? Next, will local people receive any awards? Recognition of hometown personalities has general appeal.

Example: "Little Town's own Johnny Jones will be honored at a dinner meeting tomorrow.

"Jones, a life time resident of Little Town, will be recognized as the state's leading typewriter salesman. He sold more machines last year than any other salesman in Missouri.

"The meeting will be held at the offices of Little Town Typewriter Company. More than 30 salesmen . . ."

4. *New models.* Improvements of products are news. They de note progress. They show trends.

Be sure your copy points up the affect on John Q. Public.

Example: "The large, heavy television set will soon be a thing of the past," according to Irv Levenson, Vice President of T.V. Products, Inc. "Our new set features a large screen with a minimum of mechanical parts. It can be hung on a wall, like a picture.

Levenson stated, "This will change the living habits of many families. Instead of one recreational room in each home there will be several. Our low priced set will be placed on the wall of every room in the home.

"Levenson is here for a meeting with . . ."

5. *Company growth.* Success stories are both interesting and inspiring. The growth of your company could serve as the basis of a news release, the sales meeting mentioned incidentally. News papers continually seek stories related to the American free enter prise system. Corporate growth can easily be woven into such a story.

Example: "America is still a land of opportunity. The Foster Tool Company is ample proof.

"Foster Tool was founded five years ago on a capital investment of only $2,500. Today the company is grossing $100,000 per month.

" 'Anything is possible in this wonderful country of ours,' vowed Jack Foster, company president. 'We're really just getting started'

"Foster is here for a meeting with distributors of Foster Tools. The meeting will. . . ."

6. Current *news.* Some phase of the company operation can be related to current business trends.

*Example:* "Retail sales are off 15 percent this year. Yet Wesley Manufacturing has had a 20 percent increase in sales.

# HOW TO PUBLICIZE YOUR SALES MEETINGS 153

" 'Good customer service is our secret of success,' reports Charles Morgan, President of Wesley. 'Our sales are up because customers like our service.'

"Some 30 employees of the company will convene here tomorrow to learn still more about customer service. The meeting. . . ."

### HOW TO TIME YOUR NEWSPAPER RELEASES

A good press agent never fires all his guns at one time. If he did, the newspapers would publish only one story.

Your first release should be given about three weeks prior to your meeting. It could be simply an announcement of a large sales meeting or convention. Specify the place, date, and number of people expected. You should also include the name of the person in charge of arrangements.

A second release should be given one week before the meeting. The date and place should be repeated. But new information should be included. For instance, you could name the principal speaker, his subject, his background.

The third release should be published one day prior to the meeting. Arrival of the principal speaker and newsworthy quotes are suitable. Theme of the meeting and other details should also be included.

### HOW TO PREPARE YOUR NEWSPAPER RELEASES

Give your release a professional appearance. Make them look deserving of the news column instead of the waste basket. All releases should be typed. Handwritten copy doesn't have a ghost of a chance! The editor must give handwritten copy to a reporter to type. Standard procedure is to put it in "File 13" instead. Use plain white paper. Double space your copy, using only one side of the paper. Leave 3 inches of space at the top so the editor can write his headline on your copy. This makes the editor's job easier. It spares him from reaching for shears and paste pot.

Assign a release date. This gives all newspapers an even break. It assures that every paper using your story will publish it on the same day.

## 154 HOW TO PUBLICIZE YOUR SALES MEETINGS

When no release date is specified, you get less publicity. One editor may run the story on Tuesday, while another saves it for Wednesday. The latter is "scooped." So he scraps your story. Something previously printed in a rival newspaper is of much less value.

Put your name and telephone number on every release. The editor may want to contact you for further details. Besides, he wants a record of the source. It's good protection for him and his paper. To submit a story without giving your name is like sending an unsigned letter.

### A. CITY DESK RELEASES

#1—For release three weeks before meeting.

---

FROM:  JOHN BROWN
Sales Meeting Publicity Chairman, Ajax Manufacturing Company
Lakeside 1-0708

For release Friday, July 6

One of the nation's largest hardware companies has again chosen Toledo as the site for a regional sales convention, it was announced today. More than 100 sales representatives from 12 states will be guests of the city for a two-day convention opening Friday, July 27 at the Civic Auditorium. A committee of local hardware executives, led by William Derrough, is in charge of arrangements.

### A. CITY DESK RELEASES

#2—For release one week before meeting.

---

FROM:  JOHN BROWN
Sales Meeting Publicity Chairman, Ajax Manufacturing Company
Lakeside 1-0708

# HOW TO PUBLICIZE YOUR SALES MEETINGS

For release Friday, July 20

James Truett of New York, president of Ajax Manufacturing Company, will fly to Toledo to address a two-day convention of hardware dealers opening Friday, July 27, at the Civic Auditorium. Mr. Truett, who began his career as a newsboy and now heads one of the country's largest hardware factories, will address more than 100 dealers from 12 states. Mayor Thomas Anderson will open the meeting officially Friday, and Mr. Truett will speak at a banquet Saturday evening.

### A. CITY DESK RELEASES

#3—For release the day before meeting opens.

---

FROM:   JOHN BROWN
Sales Meeting Publicity Chairman, Ajax Manufacturing Company
Lakeside 1-0708

Toledo will play host tomorrow and Saturday to a regional convention of more than 100 hardware dealers, who will hear an address by James Truett, president of Ajax Manufacturing Company. The convention will be held at Civic Auditorium, and Mayor Thomas Anderson will welcome delegates to the city at the opening session at 10 A.M. tomorrow. Mr. Truett, of New York, arrived in Toledo today. He recently toured Western Europe with other American sales executives. They told our allies how dynamic sales practices could bolster their economies. On his arrival here, Mr. Truett reported that "Salesmanship ranks with statesmanship in keeping America free. No economy is secure," he said, "unless it can sell its products, as well as its principles, to other nations of the world. America has been highly successful in selling both, which accounts for our economic and moral leadership in the world today."

After Mayor Anderson's welcome tomorrow, hardware dealers will attend a workshop session at which new sales techniques will be studied.

Saturday also will be given to shirtsleeve sessions. The convention will adjourn Saturday night after a formal banquet, at which Mr. Truett will be principal speaker.

# 156 HOW *TO PUBLICIZE* YOUR SALES MEETINGS

### HOW TO SUBMIT YOUR NEWSPAPER RELEASES

These three basic releases should be taken to the city editor's desk. The best contacts are *personal* contacts. In large newspaper offices, it is not always possible to see the city editor himself. Personal contact with his assistant is usually satisfactory, however. All stories should be taken to the editor two days before the release date. This helps the editor plan his paper. It helps him make room for your story. Keep the conversation brief. You create a more favorable impression with busy newspaper men if you can transact your business quickly.

Typical approach: "Good morning. I'm John Brown. I'm handling the publicity for a big sales meeting that's coming here next week. Here's a story for you. If I can be of further help in covering it, you'll find my name and phone number on the release. Thank you."

### HOW TO GET EXTRA NEWSPAPER COVERAGE

Of course, many sales meetings need and deserve no newspaper publicity of any kind. Where publicity is desired, the three basic releases should be ample. However, on rare occasions you'll want all the coverage you can get. Extra plugs can often be obtained in the society and entertainment sections. Often a visiting executive will stay at the residence of a local friend. This should get a squib on the society page. Professional entertainment is sometimes used. Contact the entertainers or their agent. You can get a news story and picture for the entertainment page.

### B. SOCIETY RELEASE

For release during the week preceding meeting.

---

FROM:   JOHN BROWN
Sales Meeting Publicity Chairman, Ajax Manufacturing Company
Lakeside 1-0708

# HOW TO PUBLICIZE YOUR SALES MEETINGS

For release Monday, July 23

Mr. and Mrs. David Thompson, 12121 Elm Avenue, Toledo, will be hosts over the weekend to Mr. and Mrs. Sam Spade of Dallas, Texas.

The Spades are in the city to attend the Ajax Hardware Dealers' sales convention this Friday and Saturday at the Civic Auditorium. The Thompsons and their guests are partners in several hardware stores.

### C. ENTERTAINMENT RELEASE

For release during the week preceding the meeting.

---

FROM:   JOHN BROWN
Sales Meeting Publicity Chairman, Ajax Manufacturing Company
Lakeside 1-0708

For release Tuesday, July 24

Accordionist-singer, Bobby Wilson, will top the list of entertainers appearing in Toledo Saturday night at a banquet closing a two-day convention of Ajax Hardware Dealers.

More than 100 delegates from 12 states will hear the youthful entertainer, who is a graduate of Central High School and lives with his parents, Mr. and Mrs. David Wilson, at 1304 Harvard Avenue.

### HOW TO PUBLICIZE YOUR SALES MEETINGS

**Devise Promotional Leaflets**

**Send Promotional Letters**

**Get Newspaper Publicity**

**Use the Six Major News Angles**

**Time Your Releases**

**Prepare Professional Releases**

**Submit Releases in Person**

# 16. How to Conduct Special Type Sales Meetings

### I. The Problem Solving Conference

Most sales executives don't enjoy problem solving conferences. That's because they don't like problems.

Good sales leaders are promotional minded. They're creative. They're organizers and producers. Thus, they don't enjoy "fence mending." They want others to do the problem solving.

But problem solving cannot always be dumped in the lap of a subordinate. The difficulty may be of paramount importance. Sales may suffer sharply if a solution is not effected. Therefore, problem solving conferences cannot be shirked.

"What the devil are we going to do about slow moving items?" This is the way many problem solving conferences are begun. But there's more to conference procedure than asking a few others for their opinions. There's a standard conference procedure to follow.

#### HOW TO CONDUCT A PROBLEM SOLVING CONFERENCE

1. State *the* problem. Be sure it's a single problem, small enough to be tackled. Time is often wasted in the discussion of a complex problem which involves several other problems. If necessary, break the problem into smaller segments. Then go to work on the segment that can be most easily solved.

There's another consideration. Do the conference members have authority to settle the matter? Do they have authority to

## HOW TO CONDUCT SPECIAL SALES MEETINGS 159

effect the solution they hope to reach? If the matter is above their scope of authority, the boss should join the conference.

2. *Get the facts.* All pertinent facts should be developed. When it's difficult to make a decision, it's because some of the facts are missing. The facts will clearly point toward the right solution when all the facts are known.

Opinion will often be presented as fact. Don't accept it. Ask the contributor, "Wait—is that fact or opinion?"

For full development of each fact, ask the why of it. It might be factual that the advertising department has failed to advertise slow moving items. But why? There's a reason for everything. Seek the why of each fact so you can get to the crux of the matter.

3. *List possible solutions.* Don't worry about order of importance. List them as they arise. And list all of them.

A proposed solution may at first seem impractical. Accept it anyway. Your own opinion cannot take precedence over that of conference members. If you're to regulate opinion there's no need for the conference!

Some proposed solutions may be only partial solutions. It makes no difference. Accept them anyway. They may later be amended or two of them put together.

4. Select *the most likely solution.* Usually there's discussion, if not argument. But in due time there should be agreement as to the best possible solution.

Sometimes you must change a proposed solution in order to get agreement. Do whatever is necessary to produce a "meeting of the minds." For instance, the most popular proposed solution might be "Switch to weekly deliveries." If necessary, this could be changed to "Switch to deliveries each Monday."

This step is the pay off. Push hard for it without forcing your own opinion on the others.

If a decision cannot be reached, it's usually because more facts are needed. How can you get them? Who has them? If necessary, adjourn until this additional information can be obtained.

5. *Effect the solution.* Having selected the most likely solution, put it into effect. Give it every opportunity to work. It may not be "letter perfect," so minor variations may be necessary.

If it doesn't work, select the next most likely solution. Then give it a chance to solve your problem.

If the problem still exists, continue until all possible solutions have been tried. One of them should take care of the matter.

#### 20 WAYS TO BE A GOOD CONFERENCE LEADER

1. Anticipate needs. Before the conference get all the data you think may be needed.

The discussion can go off in any direction. Even a guided discussion can take unexpected turns. So have all the files at hand. It will save time.

2. Eliminate interruptions in advance. It's folly for a dozen people to be idle while one person talks on the telephone.

"I simply tell our switchboard operator that none of the conference group will accept calls during the time of the meeting. This saves a lot of interruptions," said a Florida businessman.

3. Have an open mind. If you don't, why hold a conference?

If an employer is determined that things will be a certain way, there's no need for a conference. Merely an announcement will serve the purpose.

4. Get them acquainted. Be sure all conference members have met each other. A friendly atmosphere relaxes everyone. Be sure to create it.

5. Try to analyze. Break down the problem so you won't have more than the group can handle.

Many subjects are too broad for an effective problem solving conference. Other problems may be beyond the scope of authority of the conference group. Always analyze the problem to determine if it is appropriate.

6. Stay alert. Quick thinking is a must. Day dreaming can cause the conference leader to be caught off guard.

7. Accept all contributions. The fellow who's not permitted to throw in his 2 cents worth will be miffed. Perhaps his comment is unimportant to everyone else. But it's important to the person contributing it, so let him say a few words.

8. Keep on the track. Tangents are often interesting but sel-

# HOW TO CONDUCT SPECIAL SALES MEETINGS

dom profitable. Virtually every conference will wander out into "right field" if permitted to do so. You, the leader, must keep the discussion aimed in the right direction.

9. Refrain from squelching anyone. It doesn't pay! If someone gets out of line the others will take care of him.

10. Avoid sarcasm and ridicule. People don't appreciate it. While it makes a guy feel superior to belittle one of his conference members, it's nothing short of professional suicide.

11. Use tact. Many people wear their feelings on their sleeves. It's easy to offend a person when speaking to him in front of others.

How you treat a conference member is important. But *how he feels* you've treated *him* is even more important.

12. Let them save face. When one conference member gets "crucified" by another, put in a good word for the loser. Help save at least part of his face.

13. Have a sense of humor. An occasional laugh improves the "climate." So be ready to laugh, especially at yourself. "I have two or three jokes ready in advance," said a Minneapolis conference leader. "I work them in when things start getting stale."

14. Consider early departures. Certain participants may have special interests or qualifications. Make them feel free to leave after they are no longer involved.

15. Keep it moving. No one else is concerned about the progress of the conference. Be sure that you are. Even the brass should not be permitted to bog down the proceedings. You must keep it moving at all costs.

16. Subordinate your own opinion. Give your ideas. But consider them no more important than those of any other conference member. A Texarkana sales manager said, "Nothing is worse than a conference leader who places his opinion over that of others. He's taking unfair advantage of his position."

17. Remain in charge. Either you run the conference or others do. Don't let it "get out of hand."

18. Have only one speaker at a time. Side conversations are undesirable since those involved do not hear what is being said in the conference. A good way to stop a side conversation: "Can everyone hear what Mr. Jones is saying?"

19. Get distribution of discussion. Everyone should participate. One or two should not be permitted to hog the show.

20. Push for a solution. Little has been accomplished until the problem is solved.

Ever seen a guided missile seek out its target? It's relentless. A good conference leader is much the same way. He pursues his target, a solution, refusing to be thwarted en route.

## II. The Workshop

A group of bakery owners met for the first time. It was an enjoyable meeting. The fellows were glad to get acquainted with each other. Also, the program included some interesting speakers. They returned to their homes with the feeling that it had been a good meeting. In some ways it had. But little had been done to solve the problems of the industry. Little had been done to improve the industry. Instead, there had been a succession of speeches that superficially stabbed at a few festered places, not nearly reaching the core.

The next year they met again. This time they noticed that extra curricular conferences were quite profitable. As one bakery owner explained it, "After the meeting I spent an hour with four other fellows. They have the same problems as I do. I got more help from that one hour than I did from the two-day meeting."

The group soon realized that long-winded speeches were ineffective. One baker said, "Let's get to the crux of things. Let's solve some of our problems together. We can help each other."

Another chimed in, "Yes, and while some of us confer on one problem, a second group can discuss another matter. We might have several sections, each working on a separate problem."

Thus a workshop was born.

### HOW TO ORGANIZE A WORKSHOP

A workshop is a meeting in which people solve their own problems with a minimum of outside assistance.

# HOW TO CONDUCT SPECIAL SALES MEETINGS 163

It is a work session rather than a series of speeches. Leadership teams are drawn from the group itself. The people learn together as a result of their own efforts.

To organize a workshop, plan a general assembly as your first event. At this assembly, the group decides which problems to tackle. Make suggestions. Guide when necessary. But create the impression that they're making the decision.

### PROBLEMS CAN BE OF A POSITIVE NATURE

Not all the problems must concern things that are wrong. Some may be of a positive nature. The following are positive rather than negative:

"What can dealers do to get more business via the telephone?"
"How can better use be made of direct mail?"
"How can customer service be improved?"
"What new promotions would be timely and profitable?"
"What additional items could be merchandised successfully?"

### MOST PEOPLE WILL SUGGEST PROBLEMS THAT ARE NEGATIVE

But a natural tendency is to suggest problems of a negative nature. Here are a few:

"What can be done about the price cutting of our competitors?"
"How can breakage in transit be reduced?"
"How can travel costs of salesmen be lowered?"
"How can accidents be prevented?"
"What can be done about Smithfield Company's complaint?"

Prior to the workshop, determine which problems are most pressing. Advance information can be quite helpful. For one thing, it indicates whether there'll be too many negative problems.

There should be a healthy balance between the positive and negative. This produces better morale and a more effective workshop. You may find it advisable to prepare a few positive problems.

They can be thrown into the hopper to offset the usual barrage of negativism.

### HOW TO APPOINT COMMITTEES

A committee should be appointed for each problem. Sometimes a problem will have more than one phase, however. In this event, it may be best to appoint a committee to work on each phase of the problem.

For example, consider the problem, "What can be done to give better customer service?" This might have two distinctly separate phases. One could involve treatment of the customer while he's in your store. The other phase might have to do with service at the customer's home or office.

For maximum effectiveness, committees should consist of four to seven people. Each member should have a knowledge of the problem. His occupation should be related to the matter. Where one is not acquainted with the situation, valuable time is lost in bringing him up to date. Even then his effectiveness is questionable.

You may have a few experts in the crowd. Spread them around. Use them as consultants.

### HOW TO CONDUCT A WORKSHOP

The general assembly is adjourned. The various committees then convene in separate meeting places.

Each committee appoints a chairman and a recorder. Their functions are exactly those implied by their titles.

Every member of each committee should be urged to give his thinking. Participation is vital.

At an appointed hour, the general assembly is reconvened. Committee chairmen read reports prepared by the recorders of their respective committees. These reports may be final. Or they may be preliminary reports, followed by more committee work.

After final reports are given, there should be a summary and evaluation in the general assembly. If appropriate, have mimeographed summations distributed.

# HOW TO CONDUCT SPECIAL SALES MEETINGS

### III. The Brainstorming Procedure

Some executives say that brainstorming is the greatest thing since sliced bread. Others say it's a waste of time. Brainstorming is creative thinking on a group basis. The group should not exceed 20 people because everyone should be brought into the "act." A chairman and two recorders are needed. Comments are made so rapidly that one person cannot record all of them. So the recorders accept alternate comments.

#### HOW TO SELECT A SUBJECT FOR BRAIN STORMING

Many subjects are suitable for creative thinking. Non-technical subjects are best. They give everyone a chance to contribute. Ideal subjects:

"How can more store traffic be created?" "What should we name our customer magazine?" "How can our merchandise be promoted in the off-season?" "What are some new methods of finding prospects?" "What new uses can be suggested for the versatile salad mixer?"

Select a subject on which originality, fresh thinking, and new ideas are needed. Avoid the complex. Further, avoid policy discussion and policy making. Brain storming is creative thinking.

#### HOW TO CONDUCT A BRAIN STORMING SESSION

The group is seated around a conference table. The chairman explains the rules.

No negative thoughts may be expressed. Absolutely no evaluation of any contribution is permitted. Statements such as, "That's ridiculous." or, "That couldn't possibly work." are strictly taboo.

It's also understood that a participant will not be held in prejudice because of the quality of his comments. Quantity of new thought is the objective—not quality.

Brain storming draws from the subconscious of each participant. Thoughts near the surface are rapidly contributed. Then the participants dig into the subconscious for new thoughts. They search their minds. The results are usually surprising!

There's another angle worth mentioning. An absurd contribution often sparks comment that's not so absurd. This may lead to an idea of still greater value.

Usually there are several people wanting to comment at the same time. Each raises a hand. He speaks only when recognized by the chairman.

None of the contributions are acknowledged. Thus comments are made in rapid succession. All stops are pulled. Imagination runs wild. It's fun!

One idea may prompt another. The second idea, then, is called a "hitch hike." A participant with a "hitch hike" snaps his fingers. He's given priority over others with raised hands. This provides continuity of thought. It causes an idea to be more fully developed.

When ideas have been exhausted, the session is stopped. The recorders read their notes. Any other ideas are then added.

**HOW TO MAKE BRAIN STORMING PAY DIVIDENDS**

The notes are typed and given to the chairman. If he's like the average sales executive, he puts them in his desk and forgets about them. When this is done, there's no pay off.

The pay off comes from use of the information. Go over it. Go over it again. Eliminate contributions you cannot possibly use. But keep an open mind. Where there's merit, give heavy consideration.

After the list has been pared, ask a few questions of each idea remaining:

> "Can it be used in its entirety?"
> "Can it be used in part?"
> "Can its objectionable phases be eliminated?"
> "Should it be coupled with another contribution?"
> "Should its use be discussed with others?"

Unless you can say "yes" to at least one of the foregoing ques-

# HOW TO *CONDUCT SPECIAL* SALES MEETINGS 167

tions, the idea under consideration should be scrapped. Consider each of the ideas on your list. Among them, there may be a Jewell

### IV. The Buzz Session

In most sales meetings, participation is quite desirable. That's why it has been stressed throughout this book.

The buzz session is a splendid means of getting participation. It's chief use is in breaking a large group into several smaller groups so that individual participation will be physically possible. It gets the timid fellow in the "act/" prevents a few loudmouths from hogging the show.

An entire meeting may be constructed around the buzz session technique. On the other hand, a buzz session can be staged as one of several events.

If you've ever heard a buzz session, you know how it got its name. The talking sounds like a swarm of bees!

A buzz session is sometimes called a "six by six," for reasons that will become obvious.

#### HOW TO CONDUCT A BUZZ SESSION

To conduct a buzz session, you should first announce the topic of discussion. It can be any subject on which discussion is desired. Then divide the group into smaller groups of about six people each. The six persons to buzz with each other can pull their chairs into a circle.

Where auditorium style seating is used, persons on the odd numbered rows can turn around to face the people behind them. The six persons must necessarily face each other. It's essential for understanding.

Give the groups about six minutes in which to elect their chairman and discuss the topic. A chairman should get participation of all members of his group. When the allotted time has expired, call a halt to the buzzing. Then ask the chairmen to give their reports. It's that simple. For best results, however, you should tie the reports together. Summarize. Draw conclusions, being sure to thank the participants.

## HOW TO GIVE BUZZ SESSIONS AN INTERESTING TWIST

The opinions voiced in each small group are not ordinarily recorded. Buzz sessions are not that formal.

But an interesting twist was given at a buzz session of specialty salespeople. Chairmen were given two pieces of paper with a carbon between them. Opinions of their respective groups were recorded in duplicate. When the buzzing was stopped, the carbon copies were collected. Then came a 20-minute period in which the chairmen made verbal reports.

Two stenographers were in an adjacent room. During this twenty minutes they cut stencils based on carbon copies of the reports. They rapidly ran the stencils on a mimeograph machine. By the time the last chairman had reported, there was a mimeographed job of the entire proceedings. The stenographers actually brought the mimeographed sheets into the room before the last chairman finished his report! Every person in the room was given a copy. Every person was surprised, too.

### HOW TO CONDUCT SPECIAL TYPE SALES MEETINGS

**I. The Problem Solving Conference**

>State the Problem
>Get the Facts
>List Possible Solutions
>Select the Most Likely Solution
>Effect the Solution

**II. The Workshop**

>Plan a General Assembly Select Both Positive and Negative Problems Appoint Committees to Tackle Problems Recall the General Assembly for Reports

**III. The Brain Storming Procedure**

>Select Non-technical Subjects
>Permit No Negative Comments
>Let Imaginations Run Wild
>Evaluate Contributions Late:

# HOW TO CONDUCT SPECIAL SALES MEETINGS

**IV. The Buzz Session**

>Announce Topic of Discussion Divide People Into Groups of Six Allow Six Minutes for Discussion Accept Reports of Chairmen Summarize and Draw Conclusions

# 17. How to Conduct a Recruiting Meeting

Many companies use sales meetings as a means of recruiting sales people. For instance, nearly all of the direct selling companies conduct recruiting meetings, because recruiting is the life blood of direct selling. There must be constant, continual recruiting. Therefore, companies selling through outside sales people usually conduct regular recruiting meetings.

You've heard of such companies. Their salespeople have knocked on your door. Here are the products they sell:

| | |
|---|---|
| Special insurance policies | Albums |
| Mutual funds | Photograph coupons |
| Vitamins | Pre-need cemetery plots |
| Cosmetics | Real Estate promotion |
| Brushes | Freezer food plans |
| Housewares | Cookware |
| Water softeners | Chinaware |
| Books | Silverware |

Mass recruiting requires a great degree of skill.

In effect, a recruiting meeting is a group selling job. Instead of selling a product or service, you sell a business opportunity.

*The Gist objective in staging* a recruiting meeting *is to get* prospective salespeople to attend. *Unless there's an* audience, *it's all to no avail.*

An officer of the National Association of Direct Selling Companies stated, "A recruiting meeting can be no more successful

# HOW *TO CONDUCT A RECRUITING MEETING*　　171

than the promotion of attendance for it. There's no reason to kid ourselves. It's difficult to get prospective salespeople to attend a recruiting meeting."

### Eight Ways to Get Prospective Salespeople to a Recruiting Meeting

1. Newspaper advertising is an old stand-by. It costs money, but it gives such good results that some direct selling companies run a recruiting ad in certain newspapers every day of the year!

Most of this type of advertising is in the classified section. Display ads are so expensive they're usually reserved for special recruiting campaigns.

Your classified ad may invite the reader to write or telephone. Upon receipt of the letter or phone call, reveal as little as possible. Try only to get the individual to your recruiting meeting.

"You can't sell an opportunity by letter or over the telephone" averred a Chicago man. "If they want to smell the fragrance of a rose, they should go to the smelling place! Get 'em to the meeting. Then you can tell the whole story."

A Los Angeles lady who's an outstanding sales executive said, "When they call, I tell them nothing except the time and place of the meeting. When they ask questions, I reply with a laugh, 'You don't expect to get married over the telephone, and you don't expect to find a business career over the telephone. You'll be given *full* details tomorrow night at the meeting. It's an opportunity of a lifetime! I'll see you there.'"

Of course, other ads instruct the reader to reply by attending the meeting. In such cases, the time, date, and place of the meeting are specified.

If you're looking for anybody and everybody, your ad should simply ask the reader to show up at the meeting. If you want to qualify him, on the other hand, the ad should ask him to write or call.

"Blind" ads work best, ads that do not name the product or company. The fact that you're selling direct to the consumer should not yet be revealed. It would scare too many people away.

**172  HOW *TO CONDUCT A RECRUITING MEETING***

The following ads have worked well for certain direct selling companies:

| | |
|---|---|
| SALESMAN. For the greatest item to hit the American market in 50 years. No competition. Call FRontier 8-2010. | Distinguished person to represent distinguished product. Compensation well above average. Apply 10 A.M. on Monday at 212 Jones St. |

Why aren't earnings mentioned in the foregoing ads? Because of legal complications. When a specific figure is named you must be able to prove that your *average* salesman makes that much. Otherwise, you may have difficulty with the Federal Trade Commission.

2. The next method of getting prospective salespeople to your recruiting meeting also involves advertising.

Look under the "Situations Wanted" column in the classified section. People seeking jobs often advertise for them. Many are not seeking sales jobs, but some of them are. And some who are not will accept sales jobs if shown a good opportunity.

Contact them solely for an interview. Don't tell all in a letter or in a telephone conversation.

Be sure to hold the psychological upper hand. Don't beg them. Make them try to qualify for a chance to attend your recruiting meeting.

You already have a good opportunity. It's the other fellow who's seeking work!

Reason for this attitude on your part—you could make it sound *too* easy. The fellow who advertised thinks, "It must be one of those fly-by-night deals on a straight commission basis. It's probably door-to-door! They'll take anyone they can get, or else they wouldn't be so eager."

3. By sending postcards, bulletins or letters you can get prospective salespeople to a recruiting meeting. Two things should be considered: what does the mailing piece say and to whom is it sent?

# HOW TO CONDUCT A RECRUITING MEETING 173

Good results have been obtained with one-page bulletins. An excellent mimeographed job is okay. If the quality of the mimeographing is subject to question, use printed bulletins.

Be sure there's some art work on your bulletin. Dress it up! Further information on bulletins can be found in the chapter on "How To Publicize Your Sales Meeting."

A San Angelo, Texas, direct salesman said, "I've used postcards with good results. Try them."

---

June 16, 1960

We have several openings. If you are interested in either part-time or full-time work, report to 3609 Lynndale at 2 P.M. on Tuesday, June 21st. Please be prompt.

William Crane Hassell Company

---

To whom should mailings be sent? That's the BIG question . . .

Some companies have used the telephone directory with fair results, but nothing to scream about. Mailings are made to everyone.

You can also purchase mailing lists containing names and addresses of salespeople in your general area. To find a firm that sells mailing lists, look in the classified section of your telephone directory.

4. City directories are quite helpful. There the occupation of each person is shown. Simply check to see which people are already in the selling profession. Then direct your mailing to those people.

"It's much easier to recruit a man who's already in sales work," remarked a Cheyenne businessman. "You don't have to sell him on sales work as a career. He's already sold on it. You merely need to attract him to the opportunity in selling, that you have to offer."

People found in the city directory must not necessarily be contacted by mail. Telephone them. Or go to see them!

## 174  HOW TO *CONDUCT A* RECRUITING MEETING

5. Your sales staff can bring prospective salespeople to your recruiting meetings. Get everybody to bring a friend—or two.

Many companies pay a finder's fee. The salesman who finds another person to sell for the company is rewarded for finding him. The finder's fee might be $10 . . . or $25 . . . or more.

Under certain marketing plans, the finder receives a continuing override on sales made by people he has recruited. In such cases, however, the finder is usually responsible for training and motivating the people he has recruited.

The point is this: your salesmen know many people. They can influence some of those people to attend recruiting meetings. Urge them to do it. This is one of the best ways to build attendance.

A Tulsa man reported, "I had each of my men write down the name of every acquaintance who might like to join our sales staff. The next step was to invite the acquaintances to a recruiting meeting. I offered a prize to the man who could turn out the greatest number of his friends.

"A total of 31 new people showed up. Thirteen have been signed as salespeople! And we're still signing up people from that meeting."

6. Bulletin boards can help spread the word. Use them.

For example, there are bulletin boards in many town halls, public libraries, and state employment commissions. Supermarkets in most sections of the country are attempting to become focal points of the community. They, too, have bulletin boards.

For best results, use a printed notice. If nothing else, a typewritten notice will do.

Keep it simple. Also, keep it "blind," so as not to cheapen your product or the opportunity to represent it.

LOOKING FOR A JOB?

EITHER PART-TIME OR FULL-TIME?

CALL MR. ADAMS AT CLOVER 6-2184

An enterprising direct sales supervisor confided, "I go to real estate offices where tracts are being sold. Such an office is usually

## HOW TO *CONDUCT* A RECRUITING MEETING

located in the subdivision itself. Invariably there's a bulletin board."

He continued, "I ask the real estate people if some of their prospects argue that they cannot afford to buy new homes. Then I show how to overcome that objection. My notice on the bulletin board shows the prospect that employment is immediately available. Employment means income. It's as simple as that! I've obtained some very good salespeople in this way!"

7. Employment agencies can be quite helpful. This goes for both state and private agencies.

If your salespeople are compensated on a commission basis, you may have difficulty with a private agency. Reason: in the past they've placed salespeople who've sold little or nothing. In such cases, the agency has not received a satisfactory placement fee for its services, since it is due a percent of the first month's earnings.

There's a means of solving this problem, however. Tell the private agency, "It takes a salesperson a month or two to get started. So you won't receive a satisfactory fee on the basis of first month earnings. But collect it anyway. Then, in addition, I'll pay your regular rate on second-month earnings. The two fees should be more than ample."

State agencies are most co-operative. They'll give you names from their files. Also, they will provide a gratis desk and telephone if you care to interview applicants at the office of the state employment commission. Naturally, your proposition is made to look quite bona fide when you conduct interviews at the state office.

If there's a problem in making contact through state employment commissions, it's that the applicants are substandard. However, most direct selling companies do not expect to recruit people who are accustomed to large incomes.

8. Most cities have a Sales Executive Club. Such an organization is composed of sales supervisors from the various business firms in that town. These men band together to exchange ideas and upgrade their selling practices.

The Sales Executives Club has its finger on the pulse of sales activities in its area. When a group of salespeople are "laid off," the secretary of the Club usually knows about it. From time to time, he also knows of individual salesmen who are available. Contact the Club secretary. Better still—join the Club! In addition to recruiting, membership is helpful in many ways. The Clubs in the larger cities have placement bureaus. People looking for sales jobs may register and be placed without charge. Both members and non-members are permitted to hire these applicants. If there's a placement service in connection with the Sales Executives' Club in your city, be sure that you make the most of it.

Some of the outstanding people in direct selling have wangled invitations to speak at Club meetings. This has often resulted in prospective salespeople, either directly or indirectly.

In some cities, a direct sales supervisor of exceptional caliber has become president of the local Sales Executives Club. This has given unusual publicity to his company, his product, and the fact that he can use more salesmen.

As you can see, there are many ways to make contact with salespeople. Having made contact, you can invite them to your recruiting meeting.

At least half of those whom you expect will not appear. Why? Because the average person who needs a job is not highly motivated. If he were highly motivated, he probably wouldn't need a job!

"New York City is different from Myrtle Beach, South Carolina," averred an experienced recruiter. "In a large city, such as New York, an applicant must get to the meeting 'on his own hook/ but in a smaller town, I'd pick him up. He's much more likely to keep the 'date' if he knows I'm driving to his home to get him."

### WHERE TO CONDUCT YOUR RECRUITING MEETING

The first inclination is to stage all meetings at your place of business. That's not necessarily the best place for a recruiting meeting, however. Here's why . . .

There are signs on the doors and windows of offices. Once the visitor sees a sign, he forms an opinion. Perhaps he's driven for 30 minutes to reach the office. He may keep right on driving if, on arrival, he sees that direct selling is involved.

# HOW TO CONDUCT A RECRUITING MEETING 177

If your office facilities are exceptional and impressive, then it's a different matter. Moreover, visitors attracted by your salesmen already know something of the opportunity involved.

You might consider a hotel meeting room. The only disadvantage is in recruiting women. The ladies are a little reluctant to turn out for hotel meetings. An attractive woman stated, "I was invited to an evening meeting at a hotel and told that I'd be shown how to make $1,000 per month. I replied, "Sir, I'm a lady!"

Some Chambers of Commerce have meeting facilities. Such rooms are ideal because they make your proposition appear to be accepted by the business leaders of the city.

Y.M.C.A. and Y.W.C.A. meeting rooms have also been used to good advantage. They indicate that your business is "on the up and up" and that the people behind it are of good moral fiber. The "Y's" in Oklahoma City and Tulsa have been used for meeting rooms for many years.

## HOW TO RECEIVE THE PROSPECTIVE SALESPEOPLE

Upon arrival at the meeting place, visitors are inclined to ask questions. Some seem to be looking for an excuse to forego the meeting.

"Oh, it's canvassing? Straight commission? That's not for me!"

Station a few of your best people at the door. Advise everyone, especially those at the door, to give no information. When asked about the opportunity to be presented, your representatives should say, "We'll find out about it in just a few minutes. The meeting will start right away. Incidentally, I'm Jim Brown. And what is your name, please? I'm glad to know you, Mr. Jones. Take any chair that you like."

Most companies have the guest sign a register as he enters. This produces a businesslike atmosphere. The address and telephone number are included in registration. You are then able to make follow-up contact easily.

People arriving late will see the meeting in progress and feel that they've already missed their chance. Many will depart without attempting to enter. They're embarrassed.

Therefore, you should station someone outside the door. He can reassure them, usher them in though the meeting is already in progress.

"For a year or more I lost most of the late comers" stated a St. Paul house-wares executive. "I finally realized that many were too shy to barge in. A fellow looking for work is on the defensive anyway.

"Now I have someone outside the door. We're definitely getting some people we might have continued losing."

#### HOW TO PLAN A RECRUITING MEETING

Most direct selling organizations have a company song or two. But don't plan singing in connection with a recruiting meeting. It will seem childish to the visitors.

A two-fisted salesman said, "A certain company started its meeting by having us all join hands and sing 'The More We Get Together.' I wanted to throw up! It was not only my first meeting with that organization. It was also my last!"

Group singing can come later. Get the visitor signed as a salesman. Let him start selling. Give him time to get acquainted with your product. Then he may be willing to sing its praises.

Another common mistake is in emphasizing the product at the outset. The visitors don't like it!

They reason, "We didn't come here to be sold some merchandise. We came here to see about work. What would we have to do, what kind of work? How much will we make?"

For best results, (1) talk about the opportunity first. Hit the high spots only. Then (2) bring in the product. Next, (3) present some success stories. And (4) close with an appeal for action.

Here's a sample agenda for a good recruiting meeting:

#### SAMPLE AGENDA

### Step One: *The Opportunity.*

"Good evening. I'm Bill Newman. My name is not important but here's something that is.

"We have a tremendous opportunity to offer certain qualified people. In due time, we can determine whether you're qualified. But first, let's see what this opportunity consists of.

"We don't know exactly what you're looking for. Perhaps one of you would like to have one type of work, while another person here this evening wants something entirely different.

"But *it I* were sitting in your chair tonight, these things are the things *I'd* be looking for:

> What is the company concerned? Who owns it? Where is the main office? When was it established? Where is it doing business? What is its growth record? What is its reputation? Has it received any publicity? What job might it have for me? At what rate of pay? Is it permanent work? Is there a chance for advancement?

"Those are twelve good questions, and you're entitled to the answers. Relax, light a cigarette if you care to, and I'll give you the answers now."

No more than 15 minutes should be devoted to the answers. Use some visuals to keep interest. For example, in talking about the company's reputation you might show your Better Business Bureau membership certificate.

## Step Two: *The* Product.

"Naturally you'll want to know about the product on which this opportunity is based. Probably these are the things you'd like to know: What is the product? How does it work? Does it serve a genuine need? Will it sell? Does it have competition? Is it priced right? Is it advertised? Will it be in demand tomorrow? "Okay—let's see how our product measures up. Let's see how it answers those questions."

A brief sales presentation will do much toward supplying the answer. In addition to telling, show and demonstrate. Hold it to 15 minutes.

## Step Three: Success Stories.

"So, as you have seen, we have a tremendous product, as well as a wonderful company behind that product.

"But what about others who've tried to sell it? Have they succeeded? Well, frankly, some have not. They could have, had they tried. But our sales plan will work for you only if you will work for it.

"I'd like for you to meet some of the people who have been successful.

These men are happy in their work, they are making good money and they have splendid futures ahead of them.

"The first fellow on whom we'll call, has been with us for eight years. He lives at 3609 Lynndale here in Capitol City. Some of you may know his father who has been Cashier of the Second National Bank here for quite a long time. Let's have a big hand for one of our leading salesmen—Mr. *Elmoie Adams!"*

About three snappy success stories should take no more than 15 minutes. Be sure your speakers are rehearsed. They should stick to the theme of "here's what I've been doing, it's both enjoyable and profitable, you can do it, too."

### Step Four. Close With Appeal

"By this time you're probably thinking, 'Okay—I'm sold! This *is* it! How can I get in on it?'

"But the opportunity to represent our company is not extended to everyone. We must first learn more about you.

"That's why we have these tables and chairs along the sides of the room. As soon as we've dismissed the meeting, you can take a seat at one of those tables. Someone will come over to help you. He will ask you a few questions, and if you're lucky, he'll give you an opportunity to start working with us.

"Yes, the fellow who can join our organization is lucky. Let's hope that you are.

"Don't worry about what it will cost you to come into this business because the big thing is not what it costs to come in. The big thing is what it can cost you if you *don't* come in.

"Because this can mean all the things you've ever dreamed of—a substantial bank account . . . security . . . freedom from worry . . . a college education for the children . . . the new home on the hill.

"This is *it*. This is *really* it. If you ever find anything better than this, pick up the phone and call me collect, because I'd like to know about it!

"What you decide is up to you. The decision is yours. And the results of that decision will also be yours."

This type of close can be made in five minutes. Thus, your program lasts less than an hour. Anything over an hour long tends to lose some of its punch.

Note that the visitors were told exactly what to do to be recruited (take chairs at the tables). Many recruiting meetings

# HOW TO CONDUCT A RECRUITING MEETING

have been spoiled by failure to give specific instructions. Always let the visitors know what action to take.

### How to Hold the Psychological Upper Hand

But don't beg them to take that action. If you do, it boomerangs!

The visitor reasons to himself, "It sounds to me like they'll take anyone they can get. I've applied for jobs before but never been begged to take one of them. Apparently they profit if you're successful at this work, but they don't lose if you're not. That's why they'll take anybody and everybody. This is no good."

Therefore, speak in terms of "If you can qualify," or "If you can prove to us that you're the man for the job," or "If you can prove to us that you'll really get out and work."

You then are still holding the psychological upper hand. You're getting him to sign up because it's in *his* interest to do so. That's the only way he'll do it. He will never sell your merchandise as a favor to you or to me.

### HOW TO HANG OUT THE DOLLAR SIGN

There's the natural tendency to paint a picture of fat commissions. This is fine if fat commissions are in the offing. But most direct selling endeavors provide a good income—nothing more. If earnings were so exceptionally high in direct selling it would not be necessary to stage recruiting meetings.

A district manager in Boise said, "We take a realistic approach to the amount of money that can be made with our product. To do otherwise is sheer misrepresentation that will backfire on you.

"When fabulous earnings are not received, the salesman is disappointed. He loses confidence in you and your company. Then he quits working.

"The pity of it is that he initially didn't expect tremendous earnings. He grew to expect them only because he was led to believe that he could!"

"That's right," chimed in another direct salesman. "Most people don't expect huge commissions. They're satisfied with only several hundred dollars per month, some with less. So why claim they can make any more? It causes them to doubt the entire opportunity."

A Salem, Oregon, man, in one of his recruiting meetings: "Everyone writes his own pay check. Each check can be as big as you're capable of making it. This is a wonderful opportunity, but certainly not a 'get rich quick scheme.' "

Later he added, "In our business a man is paid all that he's worth. And perhaps that's why some people don't come into this business. They're afraid they'll be paid only what they're worth."

**HOW TO CONDUCT A RECRUITING MEETING**

**Concentrate on Turning Out a Crowd**

**Carefully Select Your Meeting Room**

**Receive Visitors Properly**

**Use a Four-Step Agenda Hold the**

**Psychological Upper Hand**

**Hang Out the Dollar Sign**

# 18. How to Conduct a Large Meeting or Convention

Sooner or later you may be faced with the responsibility of staging a large meeting or convention. Don't fight it. There is no need to do so. Stage it. Large conventions can easily be arranged.

Large conventions are like small meetings. There's but one major difference—you should delegate responsibility. Because you're the general chairman, it does not follow that you must do all the work. It's a weak executive who tries to handle everything himself. If he's not weak when the convention begins, he will be weak before it's over!

One person cannot stage a large convention by himself. It's impossible. Get other people to help. Organize, deputize, and supervise. None of them can do their parts as well as you or I, but arrange for their help anyway!

### HOW TO MAKE ANOTHER PERSON RESPONSIBLE

Appoint a chairman for your steering committee.

"It's like getting someone to stage the convention for you," said a corporation president. "Make him completely responsible. It will save you some real trouble."

The truth of the matter is that such an appointment will save you some real trouble provided you appoint a capable person as chairman. Select one of your best men, one who is dependable and tireless.

Will the man selected have ample time for the task? If not, can his regular workload be lightened? This point is important. Your steering committee chairman should not be so handcuffed with routine work that his convention activities are neglected.

#### HOW TO SELECT A STEERING COMMITTEE

The steering committee chairman will also need help in the form of a committee. Each committee member should head a major activity. The number of committee members will depend, then, upon the number of major activities.

Every convention is different from all others. Normally, though, there are six or eight major activities:

| | |
|---|---|
| Physical Arrangements | Registration |
| Budget and Finance | Reception and Entertainment |
| Promotion and Publicity | Program |
| Decoration | Banquet |

Sometimes there's need for transportation or for wives' activities.

Having determined which activities are involved, you and your steering committee chairman should select a good man for each. Then call a brief meeting. Explain to these fellows that they are members of the steering committee. Then designate them as heads of the major activities. For instance, one will be chairman of the physical arrangements, another will be chairman of the budget and finance committee, and so on.

Let them know that they may need assistance, and from where such assistance should come. For example, the chairman of the registration committee cannot personally register everyone attending a large convention. So tell him to determine his personnel needs. Let him know whether he's expected to appoint committee members from his own staff or from some other source. Then provide the head of each activity with a check list that covers many of the things he and his committee should do. These check lists need not be complete, but the head of each activity should add things to his list as they come to his attention.

**SAMPLE CHECK LIST Check List for**

**Physical Arrangements Committee**

Check One

1. Should a hotel be asked to set aside a number of rooms for people from out of town who will spend the night? .............................................................. Yes No

2. If rooms are set aside, has the registration committee been notified? The promotion and publicity committee, the reception committee?............................ Yes No

3. Is the meeting hall large enough? ........................... Yes No

4. Will there be sufficient chairs?................................. Yes No

5. Can the audience be seated with their backs toward entrances and exits so that late arrivals and early departures will not be too distracting?......................... Yes No

6. Has one particular committee member been made responsible for temperature of the meeting hall? ... Yes No

7. If there is no stage, can a platform be erected for the speakers? .............................................................. Yes No

8. Is a public address system provided?........................ Yes No

9. Does some member of the committee know what to do if the public address system fails to operate properly? ..................................................................... Yes No

10. Is there a speakers' stand?........................................ Yes No

11. Will blackboards, flock boards, projectors, screens, or extension cords be needed? ................................ Yes No

12. Has the building management told you whether a union operator is required?...................................... Yes No

13. Has a qualified operator been designated for each machine?................................................................. Yes No

14. Will extra projection lamps be on hand in case one should burn out? ..................................................... Yes No

15. Does projectionist understand when films or slides are to Be shown? .................................................... Yes No

16. If room is to be darkened has someone been designated to handle the light switches?......................... Yes No

17. Does operator of light switches know exactly when the room is to be darkened?.................................... Yes   No

18. When light switches are off, will there still be current in the base plugs for operation of projectors, tape recorders and/or public address system? .................. Yes   No

19. Will projectors be set up and tested before the meeting begins? ............................................................. Yes   No

20. If panels are used, has someone provided for tables and chairs on the platform? ..................................... Yes   No

21. Have name plates for identification of panel members been considered?.............................................. Yes   No

22. If questions are to be answered by panel members, should there be some table "mikes" for use by the panel? .................................................................... Yes   No

23. Should there be a portable "mike" for picking up comments from the floor?......................................... Yes   No

24. Will chairs, tables or other physical properties need to be moved as the meeting progresses? .................... Yes   No

25. Have certain committee members agreed to move properties as need arises? ......................................... Yes   No

### Check List for Budget and Finance Committee

Check One

1. Have one or more persons on the steering committee assumed financial responsibility for the convention?   Yes   No

2. Has this committee received a list of anticipated expenses from each working committee?...................... Yes   No

3. Have the proposed expenses been approved by this committee? ............................................................. Yes   No

4. If an expenditure is requested that appears to be unnecessary or excessive, will the committee requesting it be asked for justification? ....................... Yes   No

5. Has a reserve been set up for expenses which are not anticipated?............................................................... Yes   No

6. Should a registration fee be charged?......................... Yes   No

7. Has this committee recommended the amount of the registration fee to the steering committee? ............... Yes   No

8. Has the steering committee approved the amount of the fee? ................................................................. Yes    No
9. Has a budget been prepared and submitted to the steering committee for approval? ......................... Yes    No
10. If a registration fee is charged, is revenue in proper proportion to costs? ............................................. Yes    No
11. Is it understood that all convention expenses are ultimately to be paid by this committee? ............ ___ Yes    No
12. Has the chairman of each major activity been advised that the amount spent by his committee cannot exceed the amount authorized by this committee? ___ Yes    No
13. Has the chairman of each major activity been asked to obtain receipts for out-of-pocket expenditures on which reimbursement by this committee is desired?  Yes    No
14. Is it understood that any registration fees received by the registration committee are all to be turned in to this committee? .................................................... Yes    No
15. Are proper steps being taken at all times to safeguard moneys on hand? ............................................ Yes    No
16. If convention is at a hotel, has use of their safety deposit box been considered? ...................................... Yes    No
17. Has a separate checking account for convention funds been considered? ................................................... Yes    No
18. Will this committee be prepared to give a final report and accounting to the steering committee as soon as all bills have been paid? ......................................... Yes    No
19. Is it understood that any proceeds of the convention will be disposed of as directed by the steering committee? ............................................................... Yes    No

**Check List for Promotion and Publicity Committee**

                                                                          Check One

1. Should promotional fliers be mailed? ....................... Yes    No
2. Has the local chamber of commerce been informed of your convention plans? ............................................ Yes    No
3. Should releases be submitted to local newspapers? ... Yes    No

4. Will one of the talks, possibly the keynote address if given by a prominent person, be of sufficient interest to the general public that newspapers should be asked to send reporters?................................................. Yes    No
5. Has a good photographer been engaged?................ Yes    No
6. Should the photographer meet with speakers before the program begins, snap pictures then so that he will not interrupt later? ......................................... Yes    No
7. Should radio and TV publicity be sought?............... Yes    No
8. Will someone check the hotel bulletin board to see that the convention activities are properly listed? ... Yes    No
9. Immediately after the convention, will letters of appreciation be sent by this committee to speakers and others who helped, such as the local chamber of commerce?............................................................... Yes    No

**Check List for Decoration Committee**

*Check One*

1. Have committee members looked over the room to be decorated to stimulate thinking on what might be done? .............................................................. Yes    No
2. Will decorations be in accord with the theme of the convention? ..................................................... Yes    No
3. Will the previous users of the room leave some decorations you might want to use? ................................ Yes    No
4. Will the decorations being planned blend with the decor of the room—at least not sharply conflict with it? ......................................................................... Yes    No
5. Can decorations cover or hide any unattractive features of the room? .................................................. Yes    No
6. Will company banners or emblems be displayed to good advantage?..................................................... Yes    No
7. Is cost of decorating within reason? ......................... Yes    No
8. Will the effect of decorations, around the speakers' stand, focus attention on the stand rather than detract from it? ......................................................... Yes    No
9. Can the room be decorated the afternoon or evening before, and then locked, to avoid a last minute rush? Yes    No

# HOW TO CONDUCT A CONVENTION

10. Should decoration plans be checked with building management to determine if fire regulations are being observed?............................................................... Yes   No
11. Where the room to be decorated is several floors above ground, is each prop small enough to be put in a freight elevator? ................................................. Yes   No
12. Can some of the decorations be salvaged for subsequent use? ........................................................... Yes   No
13. Is a cleanup detail needed to remove decorations? .. Yes   No

### Check List for Registration Committee

*Check* One

1. Has this committee checked with the physical arrangement committee to learn if hotel rooms for out-of-town guests have been blocked off?.............. Yes   No
2. Can requests for hotel rooms be sent directly to the hotel instead of this committee, thus eliminating unnecessary work?................................................ Yes   No
3. If room requests go directly to the hotel, has the promotion and publicity committee been notified that persons requesting rooms should specify they are to attend this particular convention, so that the hotel will know they are entitled to rooms that have been blocked off for that group?....................................... Yes   No
4. Should someone on this committee handle advance mail registrations and, if so, has his name and address been reported to the promotion and publicity committee? ............................................................... Yes   No
5. Is it understood that all registration fees are to be turned over to the chairman of the budget and finance committee? ................................................ Yes   No
6. Depending on length of the convention, amount of light in the auditorium, and number of people attending—should name cards for coat lapels be worn by all? Yes   No
7. Is this committee aware that most chambers of commerce will furnish gratis lapel cards?...................... Yes   No
8. If name cards will be used, have they been ordered, and have arrangements been made for typewriters with large type to reproduce the names? ................. Yes   No

9. Have instructions been given to type names in ALL CAPITALS? ............................................................ Yes  No

10. If there will be a banquet has the banquet committee provided this committee with banquet tickets to sell? Yes  No

11. Will the program committee provide this committee with ample copies of the convention program? ------ Yes  No

12. Have the mechanics of registration been determined? Yes  No

13. Do you have a simple but effective procedure involving no unnecessary motion? ................................... Yes  No

14. Is everything within reason being done to eliminate the usual bottleneck at the registration tables? ___ Yes  No

15. Will registration be opened a full hour before the convention program begins? ................................. Yes  No

16. To further alleviate bottlenecks, should you consider registering some persons the night before the convention begins—or is this practicable? ..................... Yes  No

17. Does the chairman of this committee know that the local chamber of commerce might gladly provide one or more experienced persons to assist with registration on the day of the convention? .......................... Yes  No

18. Have members of this committee agreed to specific assignments in connection with registering guests? .. Yes  No

19. Will typewriters be needed at registration tables and, if so, have arrangements for them been made? .. Yes  No

20. Has the need for change, cash boxes, blank checks, receipt forms, pencils, common pins for lapel type name cards, and other details been anticipated? ... Yes  No

21. Will registrations received by mail be arranged at the registration tables in such a way that both time and confusion will be eliminated? ............................ Yes  No

22. Has some specific person assumed responsibility for the money that will go into each cash box? .............. Yes  No

23. If in a hotel, has use of the hotel safety deposit box been considered for safeguarding funds until they are turned over to the budget and finance committee? .. Yes  No

24. Do persons working at registration tables have a suitable answer for anyone claiming to have lost his ticket? ................................................................ Yes  No

# HOW TO CONDUCT A CONVENTION

25. Has the banquet committee advised whether (a) children will be given free place settings and permitted to eat some of their parents' food, (b) whether servings of childrens' food will be available at less than full price, or (c) whether a regular priced banquet ticket must be purchased for each child regardless of age? .. Yes    No

26. Has the steering committee advised whether any speakers or other guests are to be given special treatment at the registration tables?................................ Yes    No

27. Will the chairman of this committee be prepared to make a final accounting of cash receipts and unsold tickets to the budget and finance committee within two or three days after the convention?..................... Yes    No

### Check List for Reception and Entertainment Committee

Check *One*

1. Have lapel ribbons containing such words as "Official" or "Host" been lined up for committee members to wear? ............................................................ Yes    No

2. Have certain committee members been designated to great guests approaching the registration tables?____ Yes    No

3. Will someone ask persons who have registered to enter the meeting room, thus relieving congestion around registration tables?........................................ Yes    No

4. Will committee members serve as ushers in the meeting room?.............................................................. Yes    No

5. Can you prevent guests occupying seats in the rear before seats at the front have been filled? ................. Yes    No

6. Should all rows of seats be roped off and opened from the front as needed? ............................................. Yes    No

7. Should the various groups be assigned seating areas with signs erected for each group?............................ Yes    No

8. Have some front row seats been reserved for speakers and other participants to avoid delay in their getting to the platform? ...................................................... Yes    No

9. Has peppy music, such as military music, been considered for presentation about 30 minutes before the convention program is started?................................. Yes    No

10. Can music be used to advantage before any evening session? ................................................................ Yes   No
11. Is all entertainment in good taste, not likely to offend anyone? ..................................., ........................ Yes   No
12. Have you checked with the program committee to ascertain that entertainment will in no way interfere with meetings? ............................................................ Yes   No
13. Will transportation be needed? ................................... Yes   No
14. If meeting place is in a remote spot, should busses be chartered? .................................................................. Yes   No
15. Should special activities be planned for the wives? .. Yes   No

**Check List for Program Committee**

*Check One*

1. Has the steering committee advised as to what subject material should be covered in order to reach the over-all objectives of the convention? ....................... Yes   No
2. Have steps been taken to see that the proper material actually will be covered? ............................................ Yes   No
3. Are the best qualified persons being invited to speak and conduct demonstrations? ................................... Yes   No
4. Is it possible that the same speakers have been used so much in the past that people are tired of them? .. Yes   No
5. Wouldn't it be more effective if the speakers selected had not only done, but are still doing, the things to be covered in their talks? ......................................... Yes   No
6. Since few speakers can hold the attention of an audience for long, shouldn't most speeches be confined to ten or 15 minutes? ............................................... Yes   No
7. Have speakers been asked to forward outlines of their talks well in advance of the convention date so that duplication of material can be avoided and so the speakers will be prompted to prepare? ...................... Yes   No
8. Has a logical sequence of subject matter been arranged? ....................................................... __ Yes   No
9. Are strong speakers scheduled for the crucial spots—the last talk of the morning, the first and last talks of the afternoon, and the evening talk(s)? .............. Yes   No

# HOW TO CONDUCT A CONVENTION

10. Are programs being printed? ................................... Yes   No
11. Will the names of speakers be printed on the programs just a day or so prior to the convention so that last minute changes can be taken into account?   Yes   No
12. Has the use of panels been considered? ................... Yes   No
13. If panels are used, will a maximum of one hour be spent on any one subject in order to avoid monotony?   Yes   No
14. If questions from the audience are to be answered by panel members, will the questions be written on cards rather than verbally raised from the floor? ...........   Yes   No
15. Have cards been obtained for the foregoing purpose?   Yes   No
16. Will questions be screened so that objectionable and negative questions can be eliminated? ....................   Yes   No
17. Can panel activities be rehearsed? ..........................   Yes   No
18. Will the convention be started on time regardless of how few or many may be present? ............................   Yes   No
19. Would a door prize or two help people there on time?   Yes   No
20. Will the time schedule be upheld throughout the day? ..................................................................   Yes   No
21. Has each member of the steering committee been given a time schedule for the entire convention? __   Yes   No
22. Do you have a timing device of some sort for limiting long-winded speakers? .............................................   Yes   No
23. Should there be an invocation? ...............................   Yes   No
24. Would a welcoming or keynote address be of any value? ..................................................................   Yes   No
25. Have you determined some way to "break the ice" and at the same time start the convention with a bang? ..................................................................   Yes   No
26. Are skits being planned in order that the audience will get relief from the serious matters at hand? -----   Yes   No
27. Will each skit be short, preferably only a couple of minutes? ................................................................   Yes   No
28. Will each skit have a good moral or teaching point?   Yes   No
29. Has each skit been well-rehearsed? .........................   Yes   No
30. Will skits be placed on the program at points where relief will be most needed? ........................................   Yes   No

31. Have you considered calling a meeting of all speakers, about 30 minutes before the convention begins, for the purpose of giving them a pep talk and requesting that they speak with conviction and enthusiasm? .. Yes    No

32. Should you assign a different person to assist each speaker with last minute prop needs and the like? .. Yes    No

33. Have "outside" speakers, other than public officials, been asked to refrain from any real degree of commercializing in their talks? ........................................ Yes    No

34. Will someone on this or the reception and entertainment committee properly receive "outside" speakers—put them at ease, answer their questions, fill their last minute needs, invite them to remain, escort them out, and thank them for their speeches? .......... Yes    No

35. Wouldn't it be a good idea for two or three different people, not necessarily members of this committee, to handle emceeing chores? ................................... Yes    No

36. Does each emcee know that upholding the time schedule is a must? .................................................. Yes    No

37. Does each emcee know he should refrain from lengthy and anticlimactic comments on speeches that have been given? ...................................................... Yes    No

38. Have brief introductions been prepared for each speaker—introductions about 30 seconds long covering (a) what's it about, (b) why should I listen, (c) who says so?, ..................................................... Yes    No

39. Have the introductions been practiced? ................... Yes    No

40. Have special events, such as the awarding of trophies, been thoroughly rehearsed to minimize the confusion usually involved? ..................................................... Yes    No

41. If top brass are to assist in some way, have they been told exactly what they are expected to do? ............... Yes    No

42. Is someone responsible for getting the speakers to sit in the front of the room? ..................................... Yes    No

43. Will an emcee or the chairman of the steering committee take the stand before convention activities are closed and give credit to all who helped stage the convention? ............................................................... Yes    No

# HOW TO *CONDUCT* A CONVENTION

### Check List for Banquet Committee

Check One

1. Has the catering department been contacted so you can report to the steering committee on type and cost of meals available? ............................................... Yes    No
2. Has the steering committee, after referring to the budget, advised this committee as to which banquet meal should be ordered? ....................................... Yes    No
3. Has this committee given a conservative preliminary estimate to the caterer? ............................................ Yes    No
4. Has this committee learned whether a child's plate will be available or whether children will be given "set-ups" next to their parents? ................................ Yes    No
5. Has the registration committee been given the answer to the preceeding questions? .............,  ................... Yes    No
6. Are banquet tickets being printed? .......................... Yes    No
7. Will banquet tickets be numbered by the printer to facilitate counting the total number of tickets sold? ................................................................... Yes    No
8. Can the caterer wait until tickets have been sold before asking for the number of plates you will guarantee? ................................................................ Yes    No
9. As is standard procedure, will the caterer be prepared to serve ten percent more than the number of plates guaranteed? ........................................................... Yes    No
10. Would it be wise for you to guarantee about 10 per cent less than the number of tickets sold since the caterer will be able to serve these extra plates and since some ticket purchasers do not show up at banquets? ............................................................... Yes    No
11. Do you realize that in the past, more convention money has been wasted by setting the guarantee too high than in any other way? ............................... Yes    No
12. Will all seats in the banquet hall provide their occupants with a view of the speakers' stand and any visual aids to be used? .............................................. Yes    No
13. Have arrangements been made for a head table?----- Yes    No
14. Has the steering committee advised as to whom should be seated at the head table? ......................... Yes    No

15. Has seating etiquette been worked out? .................. Yes    No
16. Would it be well to have place cards? .... .............. Yes    No
17. Does price of the meal include the customary tip? .. Yes    No
18. Does the committee plan to provide corsages for the wives of banquet speakers? ................... Yes    No
19. If so, has someone checked to find out what color dresses they will be wearing so the flowers can be in complementary colors............................................ Yes    No

### Accidents Can Happen!

Many people have been injured at conventions. There have been accidents involving loss of limb, if not loss of life.

At a meeting in Ft. Smith, Arkansas, a chair collapsed. The occupant suffered a painful and costly broken spine. He sued and collected!

During a Los Angeles convention a saleslady fell from a balcony and broke her arm.

A fire in New Haven caused panic. Several persons were injured in the rush for the exits.

#### HOW TO PROTECT YOURSELF AND YOUR COMPANY

The building being used may already be insured, including public liability. But don't guess about it. Don't take someone's word for it. Be sure!

See your insurance broker. Additional protection may be needed. People don't sue for a pittance these days.

Besides, the cost of such insurance is quite nominal. You should never risk a convention without it.

### HOW TO CONDUCT A LARGE MEETING OR CONVENTION

**Appoint a Steering Committee Chairman**
**Determine the Major Activities**
**Select a Steering Committee**
**Convene With the Steering Committee**
**Provide Check Lists**
**Obtain Insurance**

# 19 How to Evaluate Your Sales Meetings

Just one thing more to be decided—Now that the meeting is over, was it worth while?

Every meeting should be evaluated soon after it's over for several reasons.

First, a meeting that seemed to be successful actually may have been a failure. For instance, the meeting may have been entertaining but not productive of better or greater sales effort.

"It's easy to be fooled," said a New England shipping executive. "We have some good showmen in our outfit. The meetings have always been entertaining. But, one day we faced ourselves with an honest evaluation of the meetings. Surprisingly enough, we had to admit they had little value."

A west coast lumber dealer reported a similar experience. "We finally started evaluating our meetings. We learned that many had not been necessary. A lot of man hours had been wasted. We'd conducted a meeting each Monday simply because Monday was our meeting day! Since then we've had only about half as many meetings."

Look back to determine what your meeting accomplished. It will help you in planning future meetings.

**HOW TO OBTAIN THE EVALUATION REPORT**

In some organizations, every person attending the meeting is asked to evaluate it.

# 198 HOW TO EVALUATE YOUR SALES MEETINGS

"We want the opinion of the salesman. Our meetings are strictly for *him.*" This pointed statement was made by the manager of an electronics firm. He obtains an evaluation report from every person in attendance.

Other companies get opinions from supervisory personnel only. The feeling here is that the salesman has no right to evaluate anything management does, including the manner in which it conducts sales meetings. "When the salesmen run the company, there's no need for me/' declared a sales manager.

Only you can decide which persons are privileged to evaluate your meetings. It is recommended, however, that the rank and file be asked for opinions at least once in a while.

Here are some of the rating sheets being used in business today:

**POST MEETING ANALYSIS**

Date of Meeting

1. Was the meeting successful? ............................. Yes   No
2. Was the objective made clear? ............................ Yes   No
3. Was the objective accomplished? ........................ Yes   No
4. Were the subjects well chosen? ........................... Yes   No
5. Did the meeting start and end on time? .................. Yes   No
6. Did the meeting drag at any place? ....................... Yes   No
7. Were appropriate visuals used? ............................. Yes   No
8. Was enough "how to" covered? ............................ Yes   No
9. Was the meeting climaxed? .................................. Yes   No
10. Did it leave you wanting more? ............................ Yes   No

**EVALUATION REPORT**

Date of Meeting

The meeting was superior, excellent, good, fair, poor. (Circle one.) Compared to the previous sales meetings, it was better, about the same, not up to par.

# HOW TO EVALUATE YOUR SALES MEETINGS

Subjects covered were quite timely, of some interest, poorly chosen.

Methods of covering the subjects were very good, fair, poor.

Can you do a better job because of the meeting? Explain ___

..........................................................

Suggestions for the next meeting are ......................

..........................................................

..........................................................

..........................................................

### POST MEETING REACTION REPORT

.........................
Date of Meeting

1. Tell whether you liked the meeting. ...........................

..........................................................

2. Tell why you feel this way. ..................................

..........................................................

3. Which part was the strongest? ...............................

4. Which part was the weakest? ................................

5. What could be done to improve the meetings? ................

..........................................................

..........................................................

6. What subjects do you want covered in the future? ........................

7. How often should meetings be held? ..............................................

8. Are we using the best time of day? ...............................................

9. Best time of week or month? ........................................................

10. The best place for the meetings? ..................................................

Note that the reports are not signed. This enables you to get an honest opinion from everyone! Few people will risk incurring the disfavor of their employers. "There's a lot I could say, but I have a family to feed!"

Having collected the reports, analyze them carefully. "I like all our meetings/' stated a sales trainer. "Why not? I plan them! But my own opinion is not material. What others think is the all important thing, because the meetings are for *them*. So I carefully analyze their opinions."

A few companies have appointed committees to evaluate their sales meetings. In such instances, the committees should contain a good cross-section. Here again, reports and opinions should be fully analyzed.

**HOW TO ANALYZE THE EVALUATION REPORTS**

Your analysis may uncover some surprising things. In most organizations, there are a few men who are pleased with every meeting as well as a few, who are never pleased.

But, the reactions are never exactly as you expect them to be. When they're unfavorable you're tempted to discredit them. Don't! You're probably being told the truth even if it does hurt. It's useless to have evaluation reports if they are not heeded.

Watch for trends . . . Are your meetings getting better, or worse? Is there more interest in your meetings, or less? Are you as glad to conduct them, or not?

Pay particular attention to the more important things . . .

# HOW TO EVALUATE YOUR SALES MEETINGS

Are the objectives being met? Are the men better off because of the meetings? Are *they doing* a *better job of selling because of the meetings?*

Sales meetings cannot accomplish miracles. For instance, if you were selling a hot specialty that finally became a dull commodity, good sales meetings would not solve all your problems. But meetings should help your men.

If you can't tell how much your meetings are helping the men, ask them. Analyze; then plan and conduct your meetings accordingly.

### The Best Evaluation of All

The overall performance of your sales organization is the best evaluation of all!

Are sales increasing? If not, can the meetings help effect an increase?

Are channels of communication open? Can your sales meetings serve as a means of communicating?

Are new policies and products properly introduced? Can this be done at your meetings?

Are the salespeople well instructed and trained? Can your meetings serve in this way?

Are ideas exchanged with your staff? Can meetings help in this respect?

Are your salespeople highly motivated? Can meetings help accomplish this?

Are your salespeople doing any creative thinking? Can meetings provide an opportunity for this?

Are problems readily solved? Can meetings help in solving them?

The foregoing questions cover the major areas to be served by sales meetings. Make your meetings pay off in each of these several ways.

"There's only one good reason for having sales meetings," opined a sales promotion expert with 40 years of success behind him. "That reason is for profit. Be sure that your company makes a profit on every meeting."

## 202   HOW *TO EVALUATE YOUR SALES MEETINGS*

### HOW TO EVALUATE YOUR SALES MEETINGS

Obtain Evaluation Reports

Analyze the Reports

Observe Over-All Performance

Determine Whether Major Areas of Need Are Being Satisfied

**GOOD LUCK!**

# Index

## A

Accidents, at conventions, 196
Achievement awards, presentation of, 135
Acoustics, of meeting room, 111
Advertising, for recruits, 171–172
Advertising campaigns, 134
Agenda, preparation of, 10
Agenda, sample of, 10–11
All-directional "mikes," 113–114
Analysis, post-meeting, 198
Anticlimaxes, 132–133
April showers theme, 19–20
Audiences:
    incentives for listening, 120
    informality, 118–119
    interviews with members of, 35–36
    introductions, 116
    money displays, 119–120
    music for, 116
    objectives of, 9–10
    with positive attitudes, 115–122
    schedule timing, 120
    size of, 13
    starting on time, 117–118
    timekeepers, 122
    timing devices, 121–122
Audio-visual aids:
    chalkboards, 50–51
    displays, 54–55
    film libraries, 47
    films and filmstrips, 45–50
    flock boards, 53
    generated charts, 51
    misuse, 45–46
    opaque projector, 50
    overhead projectors, 50
    prepared charts, 52
    production costs, 46
    projection equipment, 47–48
    projectionists, 49
    slap boards, 52–53
    slides, 46–47
    sources of, 47
    tape recorders, 53–54
    timing, 48
Auditorium style of seating arrangements, 109

## B

Badges, 116
Banquet committee, check list for, 195–196
Benefits, personal, from meetings, 6
Brainstorming, 5, 165–167
Budget and finance committee, check list for, 186–187
Bulletin notices, for recruiting, 174–175
Bulletins, promotional, 149
Buzz sessions, 167–168

## C

"Canned" presentations, 14
Central theme see Themes
Chairmanship, rotated for variety, 27–28
Chalkboards, 50–51
Chambers of Commerce, and meeting rooms, 107
Charts, generated, 51
Charts, prepared, 52
City directories, for recruiting, 173
Climaxing:
    achievement awards, 135
    additions to products, 134

Climaxing (Cont.)
  advertising campaigns, 134
  announcement of new policies, 133
  anticlimaxes, 132–133
  gimmicks, 136
  importance of, 131–132
  inspirational speeches, 135–136
  meditation, 136–137
  merchandising literature, 134
  new lines, 135
  sales aids, new, 133–134
  sales contests, 135
  semiclimaxes, 132
  V.I.P.'s, 137
  winners of contests, 135
  wives and sweethearts, surprise entry of, 136
Committees, appointment of, 164
Communications, improvement of, 2
Competitive instinct, use of, 32
Conference leaders, suggestions for, 160–162
Conference style, of seating arrangements, 109–110
Conferences, problem solving, 158–160
Contests, 38
Conventions:
  accidents, 196
  appointing chairman, 183–184
  conduction of, 183–196
  delegating responsibility, 183–184
  insurance, 196
  sample check lists, 185–196
  steering committees, 184
Coroner's inquest, for variety, 34–35
Corporate "characters," 43–44
Costuming, for variety, 33
Costuming, and speechmaking, 94
Courtroom plan, for variety, 31–32
Creative thinking, 5
Crossovers, in speechmaking, 103–104
Customers, point of view of, 100

**D**

Decoration committee, check list for, 188–189

Demonstration vs conversation, 16
Direct mail recruiting, 172–173
Discussion groups, 31
Displays, 54–55

**E**

Emcee see Master of ceremonies
Employment agencies, for recruiting, 175
Entertainment, professional, 35
Evaluation, of meetings, 197–202
Evaluation report, of meetings, 198–199
Evaluation reports, analysis of, 200–201
Experts, use of, 30–31

**F**

Fear, in speakers:
  advance notice, 62
  aids, 62–63
  audience placement, 65
  "big-wigs," 64–65
  breathing, 65
  cause of, 61–62
  confidence in material, 63
  dress rehearsals, 64
  introductions, 65–66
  pep-talks, 65
  practice, 63
  "refinders," 64
  requests vs drafts, 62
  rostrums, 64
  stumbling, 63–64
  typed notes, 63
  ways to combat, 62–66
Film libraries, 47
Filmstrips and films, 45–50
Finders, of recruits, 174
Flock boards, 53
Fundamentals, of selling, 96–97

**G**

Generated charts, 51
Gimmicks, for climaxes, 136
Giveaways, 42
Goals, 36
Group discussions, 9, 13

# INDEX

Group training sessions:
  approaches, sample quiz on, 146–147
  audience preparation, 139
  checks on learning, 140–141
  interest, promoting of, 142–146
  learning by doing, 140
  presentation of material, 139–140
  self-preparation, 138–139
  senses, appeal to, 141
  sugarcoating, 141–147
  true-false tests, 146–147

## H

Hitler, 45
Humor, for emcees, 127–128
Humor, in speechmaking, 81–90

## I

Ideas, exchange of, 4–5
Increase, of sales, 3–4
Informality, creation of, 118–119
Information, exchange of, 4–5
Inspirational meetings, length, 11
Inspirational meetings, size of, 13
Inspirational speeches, as climax, 135–136
Instruction and training, of sales staff, 3
  see also Group training sessions
Instructional meetings, length of, 11
Insurance, for conventions, 196
Interpreters, use of, 31
Interruptions, planned, 39
Introductions, at meetings, 116

## J

Jackpot drawings, 42–43
Jobbing or wholesale selling, 18–19

## L

Large meetings, conduction of, 183–196
Late-comers, 117–118
Law of averages, 98–99
Length of meetings, 11–12
Letters, promotional, 149–150
Literature, merchandising, 134

## M

Master of ceremonies (emcee):
  aliveness and vibrancy, 125
  anticipating pitfalls, 124–125
  apologizing, 125
  assisting the speaker, 126–127
  control of audience, 129
  credit giving, 130
  disturbances, 129
  humor, 127–128
  introduction of speakers, 125–126
  movement of meeting, 129–130
  participation, 128
  rehearsals, 124
  remaking speeches, 127
  showing personal interest, 127
  waiting for speaker, 126
Meals, arranging for, 107–108
Meditation, as climax, 136–137
Meeting rooms:
  choosing best, 108–109
  finding of, 106–107
  for recruiting, 176–177
Meetings, special type, 158–168
Mental attitudes, dramatization of, 97–98
Merchandising literature, 134
"Mikes," 30, 112–114
Mind reading acts, 33–34
Money displays, 119–120
"Money talks," 119–120
Motion pictures, 45–50
Motivation, of sales staff, 4
Music, use of, 116

## N

Name cards, 30
National Association of Direct Selling Companies, 170
National Society of Sales Training Executives, 94
Negative thinking, 163–164
Negative thoughts, of audience, 115
New models, announced at meetings, 135
New policies and programs, 2–3
Newspaper advertising, for recruits, 171–172

# INDEX

Newspaper publicity (See also Publicity)
  city desk releases, 154–155
  entertainment releases, 157
  example, 148–149
  extra coverage, 156
  news angles, 151–153
  planning, 150
  preparation of releases, 153–154
  society releases, 156–157
  submission of releases, 156
  timing of releases, 153
Notes, in speechmaking, 104–105

## O

Objectives, determination of, 8–9
One-directional "mikes," 112–113
Opaque projectors, 50
Outside speakers, 33
Over the counter selling, 19–20
Overhead projectors, 50

## P

Panel discussions, 29–30
Personnel, choice of, 12–13
Physical arrangements:
  acoustics, 111
  alien noises, 111
  anticipation of needs, 111–112
  check list, 185–186
  last minute details, 114
  meals, 107–108
  meeting rooms see Meeting rooms
  public address systems, 112–114
  seating arrangements, 109–111
Planning:
  agenda, 10–11
  audience needs, 9–10
  length of meeting, 11–12
  objectives of meeting, 8–9
  personnel, choice of, 12–13
  positive tone for, 13
  subject matter, 10
  time for meeting, selection of, 12
Policies and procedures, new, 133
Policies and products, introduction of new, 2–3
Positive attitudes, in audiences, 115–122

Positive thinking, 163
Post meeting analysis, 198
Post meeting reaction report, 199–200
Prepared charts, 52
Problems, conferences to solve, 5–6, 158–160
Product lines, additions to, 134
Program committee, check list for, 192–194
Projectors, opaque, 50
Projectors, overhead, 50
Promotion and publicity committee, check list for, 187–188
Promotional bulletins, 149
Promotional letters, 149–150
Public address systems, 112–114
Publicity:
  newspapers see Newspaper publicity
  promotional bulletins, 149
  promotional letters, 149–150

## Q

Quiz programs, 37

## R

Reception and entertainment committee, check list for, 191–192
Recruiting of sales people:
  bulletin boards, 174–175
  city directories, 173
  direct mail, 172–173
  employment agencies, 175
  finders, 174
  locations of meetings, 176–177
  money appeal, 181–182
  newspaper advertising, 171–172
  planning a meeting, 178
  psychological upper hand, 181
  reception of prospective salespeople, 177–178
  Sales Executive Clubs, 33, 175–176
  sample agenda, 178–181
Registration committee, check list for, 189–191
Rooms, meeting see Meeting rooms
Roundup theme, 18–19

## S

Sales, increased by meetings, 3–4
Sales aids, new, 133–134
Sales contests, 135
Sales Executive Clubs, 33, 175–176
Sales fever theme, 20–21
Sample agenda, 10–11
Seating arrangements, 109–111
Semiclimaxes, 132
Seminars, for variety, 28–29
Showmanship, 16, 26–44, 92–94 see also Variety
Skits, use of, 39–41
Slap boards, 52–53
Slides, as audio-visual aid, 46–47
Special type meetings, 158–168
Speakers and speeches:
   acting out, 101
   appeal to emotions, 91
   appropriateness of point of talk, 69
   audience reaction, 72–73
   basic fundamentals, covering of, 96–97
   beginning of talk, 71–72
   changes of pace, 60
   close of talk, 70
   collecting material, 68
   customer's point of view, 100
   costuming, 94
   crossovers, 103–104
   crucial spots, 59
   development of point of talk, 70
   emcee see Master of ceremonies
   fear see Fear, in speakers
   five-step plan, 71–72
   good story tellers, 81–82
   helping speakers, 60–61
   humor, 81–90
   interest-getter devices, 71
   interruptions, timely, 102–103
   law of averages, 98–99
   length of talk, 59, 79
   light and interesting talks, 94–95
   logical sequence in subject matter, 59–60
   loss or gain dramatized, 100–101
   mental attitudes dramatized, 97–98
   minimization of, 57–58
   notes, use of, 104–105
   organization, 68–79
   point of talk, deciding on, 69
   preparation for speakers, 60
   rotation of assignments, 58–59
   restatement of point, 70
   sample speeches, 73–79
   selection of speakers, 58
   showmanship, 92–94 see also Variety
   simplicity of five-step plan, 73–79
   stimulation of speakers, 101–102
   systematic prospecting, 99–100
   timely interruptions, 102–103
   voice projection, 66–67
Spotted tables, seating arrangement, 110
Stage fright see Fear, in speakers
Steering committees, for conventions, 184
Subject matter, arrangement of, 10
Suspense, use of, 38–39
Systematic prospecting, 99–100

## T

Tape recorders, 53–54
Testimonials, from salesmen, 43
Theater in the round, seating arrangement, 110–111
Theater techniques, use of, 41
Themes:
   announcements, 24
   application, 17–18
   decorations, 23
   entertainment, 23
   for jobbing or wholesale, 18–19
   language, 23
   list of, 21–23
   for over the counter selling, 19–20
   refreshments, 24
   selection, 17
Time, starting on, 117–118
Time for meetings, selection of, 12
Timekeeping, 121–122
Tone of meeting, 13–14
Training and instruction, of sales staff, 3
   see also Group training sessions
Training meetings, length of, 11
Travel expenses, 12

"Tryouts," 11, 13, 138
Two-directional "mikes," 113

## V

V.I.P., surprise entry for climaxes, 137
Variety:
  chairmanship rotated, 27–28
  competitive instinct, 32
  contests, 38
  coroner's inquest, 34–35
  corporate "characters," 43–44
  costuming, 33
  courtroom plan, 31–32
  discussion groups, 31
  entertainment, professional, 35
  experts, 30–31
  giveaways, 42
  goals, 36
  interpreters, 31
  interviews with members of audience, 35–36
  jackpot drawings, 42–43
  mind reading act, 33–34
  outside speakers, 33
  panel discussions, 29–30
  planned interruptions, 39
  quiz programs, 37
  seminars, 28–29
  skits, 39–41
  suspense, 38–39
  testimonials, 43
  theater techniques, 41
Voice projection, 66–67

## W

Wholesale selling, theme for, 18–19
Wives and sweethearts, surprise entry of for climaxes, 136
Workshop meetings, 162–164

# Also available from www.sunvillagepublications.com

**BRAIN STORMING**
The Dynamic Way To Create Successful New Ideas
Charles H. Clark

**How To Write SUCCESSFUL BUSINESS LETTERS In Just 15 Days**
John P. Riebel

**CHALK TALK MADE EASY**
A COMPLETE SELF-INSTRUCTION COURSE IN CRAYON AND BLACKBOARD DRAWING
BY WILLIAM ALLEN BIXLER "THE RILEY ARTIST"

**USING CHARTS TO IMPROVE PROFITS**

Ely Francis

**How To Help Groups Make Decisions**
Grace Loucks Elliott

**HOW TO CREATE NEW IDEAS**
A Comprehensive Course in The Art and Science of Creative Thinking
Jack W. Taylor

**How To Plan Meetings**
And Be A Successful Chairperson

Joseph G. Glass, PH.B., LL.B.

**How To Run BETTER MEETINGS**

Edward J. Hegarty

**The Successful Sales Meetings Handbook**
Bill N. Newman

www.ingramcontent.com/pod-product-compliance
Lightning Source LLC
Chambersburg PA
CBHW071417170526
45165CB00001B/313